TRIUMPH

CROWOOD MOTOCLASSICS

The Complete Story

Ivor Davies

The Crowood Press

First published in 1991 by
The Crowood Press Ltd
Gipsy Lane, Swindon
Wiltshire SN2 6DQ

British Library Cataloguing in Publication Data

Davies, Ivor *1913*–
Triumph.
1. Triumph motorcycles, history
I. Title
629.2275

ISBN   1 85223 458 X

Acknowledgements
Line illustrations by David Oliver

Dedication
Dedicated to my wife Doreen. We met at Meriden, married, multiplied
and have lived Triumphantly ever since.

Typeset by Acorn Bookwork, Salisbury, Wilts.
Printed and bound in Great Britain by BPCC Hazell Books, Aylesbury

Contents

	Preface	9
	Introduction	10
1	Bettmann's Own Story of Triumph	12
2	The Early Giants	18
3	The Bettmann Motorcycles	24
4	The Modern Era	37
5	The Rise of Triumph	43
6	The Speed Twin	50
7	War and Triumph	60
8	Triumph and America	66
9	East Coast – West Coast	80
10	Post-War Motorcycle Development	91
11	Turner Is Back	96
12	New Models	103
13	Company Upheavals	126
14	Turner Retires	132
15	Triumph Goes Racing	136
16	Managing Directors Come and Go	144
	Postscript	151
	Appendices	153
	Index	159

100 YEARS OF TRIUMPH

1883 Siegfried Bettmann comes to England from Nuremberg Germany and is employed by Kelly & Co.

1885 S Bettmann & Co Import-Export agency started in London, selling bicycles made in Birmingham.

1886 Triumph name replaces Bettmann.

1887 Triumph Cycle Co name adopted. Mauritz Schulte joins Bettmann.

1888 Small factory acquired in Coventry for manufacturing bicycles.

1889 Bicycle manufacture started. Company moves from London to Coventry.

1897 Schulte considers producing Hildebrand & Wolfmuller motorcycle under licence. Name registered as New Triumph Co Ltd but changed later to Triumph Cycle Co Ltd.

1898 Bettmann negotiates to make Humber motorcycle, but agreement not reached.

1902 First Triumph motorcycle using Belgian Minerva engine with automatic inlet valve and battery/coil ignition.

1903 Minerva engine with normal side-valve layout.

1904 J A Prestwich engine (JAP) now used, also second model with Belgian Fafnir engine.

1905 First all-Triumph machine produced, designed by Schulte and Hathaway. Production 250 per annum.

1906 Triumph Engineering Co Ltd registered 23 April 1906. Capital £100 (increased to £21,000 25 February 1936).

1908 Variable pulley – high 4:1, low 6:1 – with minimum dismantling, also 2-slide patent carburettor introduced. Jack Marshall wins single-cylinder class in Isle of Man TT Race and makes fastest lap – 42.48mph (68.36kph).

1909 Production now up to 3,000 per annum.

1910 TT model catalogued with magneto ignition only – coil not even optional. Albert Catt rides 2,000 miles (3,220km) in six days.

1911 Free engine model announced with multi-plate clutch in rear hub.

1913 Bettmann elected Mayor of Coventry. Experimental vertical twin side-valve featured in press. Two-stroke 225cc 'Junior' model announced.

1914 Model 'H' introduced, 550cc side-valve with Sturmey Archer 3-speed gearbox and chain-cum-belt transmission. Some 30,000 supplied to Allied forces in World War I.

1919 Mauritz Schulte leaves company with a £15,000 'golden handshake'. Claude V Holbrook joins as General Manager.

1920 Model 'SD' (Spring Drive) with all-chain transmission through first Triumph 3-speed, own make gearbox.

1921 500cc 4-valve OHV Model 'R' introduced. Top half designed by Ricardo – hence nickname 'Riccy'.

1923 350cc unit construction Model LS announced. First Triumph cars produced, engines by Ricardo.

1924 Internal expanding brakes on chain-driven models.

1925 500cc side-valve Model 'P' with 3-speed gearbox and all-chain drive at £42.17s.6d. causes sensation.

1927 500cc two-valve two-port OHV Model TT developed by Vic Horsman, Brooklands ace and Liverpool dealer (later).

1928 Triumph adopts fashionable saddle tank, but only on certain models. First move away from traditional green colour scheme to black with gold lines or pale blue panels on black.

1929 Annual production of 30,000 achieved.

1931 175cc Model 'X' two-stroke at £23.17s.6d. with lights and legshields.

1932 Val Page, designer, joins Triumph from Ariel. Bicycle manufacture sold. 'Silent Scout' models introduced with special cams and followers to reduce clatter.

1933 New range of single cylinders and 650 twin designed by Val Page.

1934 Name changed to Triumph Co Ltd.

1935 Model 5/10 500cc two-port racer, specially tuned, special tank, alternative pistons etc. Priory Street and motorcycle production threatened with closure. Car manufacturing plant in the Holbrooks area of Coventry acquired.

1936 Triumph Engineering Co Ltd formed. Jack Sangster buys the Priory Street works and appoints Edward Turner as General Manager and Chief Designer. Val Page joins BSA, Bert Hopwood joins Triumph. Tigers 70, 80, 90 announced.

1937 Edward Turner introduces 500cc Speed Twin at £75.

1938 Original Triumph works in Much Park Street sold.

1939 Tiger 100 announced. Tiger 90 discontinued. World War II declared.

1940 350cc twin (3TW) approved for Services. Priory Street works destroyed in Coventry blitz. Initial batch of 350 twins destroyed – end of this model.

1941 Temporary premises acquired in Warwick. 350 and 500cc side-valves in production for Services. Work on new factory at Meriden started. Turner moves to BSA.

1942 New factory at Meriden in production for military with 350cc OHV 3HW based on pre-war 3H, but improved with enclosed valve gear etc.

1944 Edward Turner back at Triumph as Managing Director.

1945 Large stocks of used 3HW and 3SW models bought from War Department for re-conditioning and selling in civilian colours.

1946 All-twin cylinder range announced – 350cc 3T de Luxe, 500cc Speed Twin, 500cc Tiger 100. Telescopic forks on all models, Spring Wheel extra. Tiger 85 twin and 3H single announced but not produced. Ernie Lyons wins Manx Grand Prix on Tiger 100.

1947 Bert Hopwood leaves Triumph for Norton.

1948 500cc Trophy (TR5) introduced following success in International Six Days Trial. Grand Prix model announced.

1949 650cc Thunderbird launched with 500 miles at 90mph (800km at 145kph) demonstration by three models at Montlhéry. Nacelle headlamp enclosure on all models.

1950 Painted fuel tanks with pressed styling bands and badges due to temporary lack of lining capacity.

1951 Triumph Corporation in Baltimore (USA) starts operating. Triumph sold to BSA for £2½M.

1952 Tiger 100, ridden by Bernard Hargreaves, wins Clubmans TT in Isle of Man at 82.45mph (132.68kph).

1953 150cc OHV Terrier introduced. Directors ride from Land's End to John o' Groat's in Terrier demonstration.

1954 Tiger 110 announced – very high performance version of Thunderbird. Swinging arm rear suspension on Tigers 100 and 110. 200cc Tiger Cub announced.

1955 Johnny Allen clocks 193mph (310kph) on Bonneville Salt Flats in 650cc Triumph-powered streamliner.

1956 Jack Sangster becomes Chairman of BSA Group. Johnny Allen achieves 214.4mph (345kph) at Bonneville.

1957 Unit construction 350cc 'Twenty One' introduced. Twenty-first Anniversary of Triumph Engineering Co Ltd.

1958 Tiger Cub with swinging-arm frame.

1959 T120 Bonneville introduced, also Tigress Scooters – 175cc two-stroke and 250cc OHV Twin.

1960 BSA Group makes record profit of nearly £3.5M in centenary year. Jack Sangster hands over Chair to Eric Turner.

1961 Bert Hopwood comes to Triumph.

1962 Doug Hele joins Triumph from Norton. Bill Johnson sets new World Record at 224.57mph (361.40kph) with 650cc stream-liner.

1963 Tiger 90, high performance 350 introduced. All 650s with new unit construction engine/gearbox.

1964 Edward Turner retires, but retains BSA Directorship.

1965 Tiger Cubs supplied to French Army, using T20S/H Sports Cub specially adapted.

1966 Bob Leppan's streamliner with two 650 Triumph engines sets new US record at 245.6mph (395.2kph). Buddy Elmore wins Daytona 200 on works-prepared Tiger 100.

1967 Introduction of twin carburettor Tiger 100 Daytona (T100T). Gary Nixon on Tiger 100 wins Daytona 200. Edward Turner retires from BSA Board.

1968 Late summer announcement of three-cylinder 750cc Trident.

1969 Malcolm Uphill, riding a Bonneville, wins Production TT in Isle of Man at 99.99mph (160.91kph) with first ever over 100mph (161kph) lap by production motorcycle – 100.37mph (161.52kph).

1970 Malcolm Uphill repeats his win in Production TT, but this time riding a Trident.

1971 BSA Group loses £8M. Lord Shawcross takes over Chair. Tridents win Production TT (Ray Pickrell) and Formula 750 (Tony Jefferies) races in Isle of Man.

1972 BSA Group loss reduced to £3.3M. Ray Pickrell wins both Production TT and Formula 750 races in Isle of Man.

1973 Edward Turner dies. BSA Group merged with Norton-Villiers as Norton-Villiers-Triumph with Dennis Poore as Chairman. Closure of Meriden works announced – start of 'sit-in'.

1974 Bert Hopwood retires. Trident production launched at BSA works, Small Heath.

1975 Trident NT160 electric-start model announced. Meriden workers co-operative set up with Government loan of £4.2M. Ten-lap Production TT won by 'Slippery Sam', fifth consecutive win of this single machine! American market shows signs of collapsing.

1977 Triumph marketing rights and assets assigned by NVT to Meriden Co-operative.

1983 Production of Bonneville continued at Meriden until 1983 when Receiver is called in.

1984 Meriden factory demolished, sight acquired for housing estate which retains links by using Bonneville and Daytona in road names.

1988 Manor Hotel in Meriden, much used years ago by the company for sales conferences and similar functions builds a new bar called the 'Triumph Bar', decorated with a photographic display illustrating the history of Triumph from start to finish.

1990 Triumph lives again, having been rescued by John Bloor. Cologne Motor Cycle Show launches new Triumph six-model range.

1991 All being well, the Daytona 750 and 1000, Trophy 900 and 1200, and Trident 750 and 900 roll off the Hinckley production line.

Preface

The story of the Triumph motorcycle is a long and fascinating one which started over one hundred years ago. It can be divided roughly into two parts – the Bettmann era and the Turner era. Bettmann began in 1885, Turner in 1936. Bettmann was German, Turner was British.

In this book we leave Siegfried Bettmann to tell his own story of how Triumph came into being. Turner's part was a rescue operation when the Bettmann organization was in danger of shutting up shop after trading for more than fifty years.

Bettmann's partners were Mauritz Johann Schulte and Col. Claude Vivian Holbrook. These three I have called the 'Early Giants'.

The man behind Edward Turner was John Young Sangster, shrewd businessman and engineer. When Bettmann's company was in difficulties, Sangster stepped in and bought it. He then put Turner (already working for him at Ariel) in charge.

Turner moved fast, produced some very saleable new motorcycles, including one that changed motorcycle design worldwide – the Speed Twin. This was *Turner's Triumph!*

Introduction

The many books written about Triumph give some indication of the impact that this marque has made on the motorcycling scene over the years. In the very early days Triumph products attained such a high degree of quality and reliability, by the standards of the day, that it is often claimed that but for Triumph, motorcycles might well have disappeared from the roads altogether. Triumph proved in no uncertain way that powered two-wheelers were a trustworthy means of transport in much the same way that George Stephenson's 'Rocket' of 1830 demonstrated that the steam locomotive was a practical machine for moving loads on a railway.

In this book, the emphasis is largely on the period when Edward Turner was Managing Director. When, with Jack Sangster, he took over the bankrupt Triumph Company Ltd in 1936, he was faced with the monumental problem of getting the company on its feet again. This he did in a spectacular manner, with brilliant new products which won immediate acceptance by the buying public. He also recognized the potential of the USA as a market and I am privileged to reproduce in this book some very interesting correspondence between Turner and Bill Johnson Jnr of California in which the creation of this market can be traced. From being virtually non-existent, the USA market eventually absorbed a quantity that represented a major part of the Meriden factory's output – and would have taken more if production could have coped.

This book is not all about Turner though. Siegfried Bettmann, the man who started it all in Good Queen Victoria's reign, tells his part of the story in his own words. You may well find reading this, that the problems and difficulties he encountered then were very similar to those we experience now. He even complains about the depreciated pound!

In addition to Bettmann, Turner and the other leading figures in the Triumph story, I have made mention for the first time of many others employed by the company who all played a vital part in the Triumph saga. No doubt I shall be criticized for leaving out Bill So-and-So and Mary-you-know-who, but this is a risk I have had to take; it is no reflection on all these other equally worthy characters – unfortunately, there is a limit to the space available.

Historic comparison! The very first Triumph, 1902 2¼hp with Minerva (Belgian) engine alongside probably the most popular Triumph of all, the Bonneville (this one from 1960).

Ariel, BSA, Carbodies and Daimler come into the story too, as they were part of the BSA Automotive Division along with Triumph. Edward Turner was Chief Executive of the Division, so all four companies were to some extent associated.

I offer my apologies to those copyright holders of some of the older photographs, where efforts to contact them have failed.

Ivor Davies

1

Bettmann's Own Story of Triumph

26 May 1949

Before Mr Sangster left for his world tour he wrote to me on 6 January 1949 and asked me to write up a short history of the Triumph Company from its inception in 1885 until 1936, and he said at the same time that three or four pages would serve the purpose.

It is difficult to describe the history of the Triumph Company in such a short space as it forms in reality a large part of my life. I shall try to comply with his wishes as far as I can. Let me therefore begin with the fact that I came to this country in November 1883, when I immediately looked out to find a situation, answering all the suitable advertisements which appeared in the *Daily Telegraph*. After a fortnight I was successful and was engaged by Messrs Kelly & Company at a weekly wage of 25/- [125p]. Messrs Kelly & Company were, and I believe still are, the editors and publishers of the London Directory and they also publish numerous foreign directories containing the names of firms whose acquaintance might be of practical interest to English business men and manufacturers.

My work was to compile out of foreign directories a suitable collection of such firms for their (Kelly's) publications. I tried to improve my position, and after six months I had the luck to be engaged as foreign correspondent by the White Sewing Machine company, an important firm of sewing machine manufacturers of Cleveland, Ohio, who had a branch in London in Queen Victoria Street. Here, I may say, began the history of the Triumph Company.

After three or four months I induced the manager of the company, Mr George Sawyer, to employ me as his traveller in foreign countries. In this way I began to know most of the European countries, also a large part of North Africa. I succeeded in gaining new customers for the company, and many of them in turn became my life-long friends who supported me in my future undertakings. After a year or so a quarrel arose between Mr Sawyer and myself, this however did not definitely break the ties of mutual friendship. I decided then to start in business on my own account by acquiring agencies of German firms amongst whom was the firm of Biesolt & Locke, who were sewing machine manufacturers at Meissen in Saxony. With the exception of this firm, the agencies proved to be a failure, although to add importance to the firm I named it S. Bettmann & Company.

It was about that time that the 'penny farthing' bicycle, with a high wheel at the front and low wheel at the back, began its successful career. This was first turned into a lower and safer machine by Mr William Hillmann, a partner in the firm of Hillman, Herbert & Cooper Ltd which later during the cycle boom became the Premier Cycle Co Ltd. Mr Hillman called his machine, which was provided with two chains, the 'Kangaroo'. This bicycle was further improved and made safer by Rudge Whitworth Limited who manufactured the 'Bicyclette' and later again by J K Starley, the owner at the time of the firm which later became the Rover Cycle Co Ltd and is now the manufacturer of the Rover car. These two machines are, or were, the prototypes of the present day safety bicycle.

When I started in business I came to the conclusion that in order to be successful I would have to distribute a machine bearing its own name, I therefore decided to approach a manufacturer in Birmingham – Mr William Andrews – to manufacture a machine for me to which I gave the name 'TRIUMPH' I chose this name for a single purpose. For a long time my customers, who were practically all on the Continent, talked of the bicycle as being the 'Bettmann'. Such a name could not be of permanent value,

Siegfried Bettmann of Nuremberg, who founded the company and gave Triumph its name.

I therefore looked out for a name which could be understood and would be understood in all European languages and so I decided to call the bicycle the 'Triumph'.

I must now mention that about two years later an excellent and far-seeing man joined me in partnership. He was M J Schulte, and our partnership lasted for many years until two or three years before the end of his life. We soon found that in order to gain a real success we had to become manufacturers; we therefore looked out for works in Coventry, which at that time was the Metropolis of the Cycle Industry. Schulte preceded me and found suitable works in Earls Court, Much Park Street. The building belonged to Mr Alderman A S Tomson, who was Mayor of Coventry seven times. We worked hard but under great difficulties, our capital was small, it simply consisted of £500 given to me by my parents and £150 which Schulte obtained from his relations. In spite of the smallness of our capital we had a certain amount of success.

A sample of the founder's handwriting.

A highly respected citizen of Coventry, Mr A E Fridlander, began to take an interest in our undertaking, he induced Mr Tomson and one other friend with himself to invest some money in our concern; this was the beginning of the Triumph Cycle Company Limited whose original capital was £2,000. Of this amount, if I remember correctly, £800 was given in shares to Schulte and me for our possessions and a great deal of this £800 must have been represented by goodwill. Then came the cycle boom, when Mr E Terah Hooley promoted cycle companies with a large capital of which I will give only one instance, this was the firm of Singer & Company. The company was floated by Hooley with a capital of £800,000 of which £200,000 were issued in five per cent Debentures, £200,000 in six per cent Preference Shares and £400,000 in Ordinary Shares. As the actual assets of the company consisted of only about £150,000 the goodwill was, therefore valued at the enormous sum of £650,000. Let me say that at that time the pound had real value and had not depreciated as at present.

I should like to give a short history of the Dunlop Tyre Company which was founded at that time in Dublin. The success of the cycle industry was due to a great extent to one remarkable man who was Mr Harvey du Cros of Dublin. A veterinary surgeon who also resided in Dublin, Mr J B Dunlop, conceived the first pneumatic tyre. Mr Harvey du Cros immediately comprehended the valuable points of this improvement and started the Dunlop Tyre Company. To give the new undertaking a further foundation he purchased the cycle business of Messrs Booth

Brothers of Dublin. I have forgotten the original amount of the company but I think it was £25,000. The success of the pneumatic tyre was enormous. One of the directors of the original Dunlop Tyre Company was Mr R J Macredy, the owner and Editor of the *Irish Cyclist*. In order to make the tyre better known also on the race track, Mr Macredy although not quite a youngster, took part in the National Cycle Union Races which embodied the championships of the cycle sport. When Mr Macredy appeared on the track they all laughed but were surprised when he romped home in front, an easy winner. [Here Mr Bettmann gives balance sheet figures that year for the Dunlop Tyre Company which we omit.]

Mr Harvey du Cros had followed with interest the activities of our small company. One day his son Arthur (now Sir Arthur du Cros Bt) called on me and told me that his father would like to make my aquaintance . . . I had an interview with Mr Harvey du Cros in Ireland's capital, when he told me that foreseeing the successful future for the Triumph Company he would like to induce his Board to support us by investing a fair amount of the surplus capital of their company in our business.

Mr du Cros sent his accountant to investigate our books and everything having been found satisfactory, the Triumph Company was reconstructed with a capital of £45,000 half of which was in Preference Shares and half in Ordinary Shares. At that time my late friend, Mr John Griffiths, was Secretary of the Dunlop Tyre Company. Mr Harvey du Cros persuaded him to purchase the businesses of the most successful cycle dealers throughout the coun-

try, and in this way the 'John Griffiths Corporation' was started with a capital, if I remember correctly, of £300,000. I persuaded Mr Griffiths to take up the agency of the Triumph bicycle for some of his depots, whilst in London we continued with the White Sewing Machine Company. During the boom the Triumph Cycle Company was turned into a public company, the capital of which was £40,000 in six per cent Debentures, £50,000 in six per cent Preference and £80,000 in Ordinary Shares. The Debentures and Preference Shares were underwritten by the Dunlop Tyre Company and were just applied for by the public. On the other hand the £80,000 Ordinary Shares were subscribed for more than ten times over, this of course was only done for the sake of speculation as most of the 'original' shareholders – amongst whom were some of my personal friends – sold them as soon as possible at any profit they could obtain.

After the boom came the slump, and in the first year of the slump our balance sheet showed a small loss of about £1,500. At the General Meeting of the Company a few shareholders kicked up a terrible row and pretended to know that the loss was entirely due to bad management. I answered them, perhaps in somewhat vehement language and Schulte tried to pull me down and told me to keep quiet. Without Schulte's or my knowledge, Mr Fridlander and Mr Tomson had considered that it would be a good thing for the company if Mr John Rotheram, one of the most highly respected citizens of Coventry at that time, could be persuaded to join the Board; they therefore, at the General Meeting of the Company, proposed that he should be an additional director. He declined but said that if the Managing Directors wished it he would be pleased to see them from time to time in order to discuss the progress of the business with them. After one year, at the next General Meeting, Mr Rotheram reported that he would resign this office as he had found by his interviews with me that the affairs of the company were in good and honourable hands.

Here I may mention that at the time I came to England, a young man from Bavaria also landed in this country, he was Philip Schloss, who was in the employ of a Nuremberg firm of toy manufacturers who intended to start a selling branch in London. Schloss was chosen to manage the branch at the time the Triumph Company was formed, he had saved £100 and it showed the confidence he had in me that he asked me to be allowed to invest his £100 in the new company. I was so pleased with getting his £100 that I asked him to become a director with a seat on the Board. Schulte agreed, but he also asked me at the same time not to be so lavish in future in the offering of directorships.

In the year 1914, when I was Mayor of Coventry, war broke out. One morning (it was a Sunday), at my private house I was called on the telephone by the War Office. The man who addressed me was Staff-Capt. Claude V Holbrook. He asked me whether I could make arrangements to get one hundred Triumph motorcycles packed immediately to enable him to ship them to France? I promised to do my best. I called on Charles Hathaway, our Works Manager, who succeeded in getting four packers together and the motorcycles left at the right time. I had

occasion to see Capt. Holbrook (who was soon promoted Lieutenant-Colonel) frequently at the War Office, and from our interviews sprang a lasting friendship. I was so impressed by his capabilities that I asked my co-directors to allow me to propose him to become the Manager of the Company. My relationship with Schulte, as is usually the case when two opposite characters have to work together for many years, became somewhat strained. My idea was that Schulte should retire, which he did on the payment of £15,000 and that Colonel Holbrook should take his place in the management of the works.

For the first few years under Holbrook's management all went well. We made one mistake when we gave up the manufacture of bicycles and handed them over to a Mr Downes who had a small bicycle factory in Coventry. When Schulte was still Managing Director he wished to get rid of the cycle business and instead of the cycle to get into the motor car trade, but this was not done until Holbrook had joined the firm. The first car we made was a great success but Holbrook, for some reason which I could never fathom, always wanted to change. A car which was successful had always to be replaced by something new and such experiments are very expensive.

One day, a Mr Newnham, who had a large motor car business in London, called on me with his son. They asked me to entrust them with the Triumph car agency for London. The mistake I made was that I not only listened to them but accepted their proposal. Mr Newnham's son, by his future conduct, did not gain my confidence, although in time he became a close friend of Colonel Holbrook.

Although under the old management the company had large sums of money at their credit in the bank and also large investments, it all disappeared and the company was obliged to obtain a considerable overdraft from the bank. I have a suspicion that Holbrook was of the opinion that I was in the way of success, without my knowledge he had arranged with the General Manager of Lloyds Bank in London to send an accountant to investigate the firm's affairs. They all – the General Manager of the bank, the accountant and Holbrook – came to the conclusion that the man who prevented successful trading was me, with the result that I had to give up the Managing Directorship and become Vice-Chairman of the Company. It was proposed that I should become Chairman, but this I declined as I did not think it fair to ask Lord Leigh to resign, although I am sure he would not have minded a bit doing so.

The improvement imagined by my successors which would follow my retirement did not take place, the result was that the bank appointed a manager, a Mr Graham. He soon concluded a kind of firm friendship with Colonel Holbrook and Mr Newnham. His first idea was to give up the motorcycle trade and to restrict the resources of the company to the manufacture of motor cars. The rumour of such proceedings reached Mr Sangster who went, as far as I know, immediately to Holbrook and asked him not to throw the motorcycle business away for nothing but to let him have it. This, as far as I can remember, was in 1936.

Mr Sangster called on me and asked me to be Chairman of the new company, to which was given the name of Triumph Engineering Co Ltd. I agreed to do so, but for some reason into which it is not necessary to go further, but which was of the most friendly character, I (soon) retired from the Chairmanship and this ended my active commercial life.

Siegfried Bettmann

2
The Early Giants

Siegfried Bettmann (1863–1951)

Triumph was Bettmann's brainchild and his initiative and drive brought the company into existence. From his own words quoted earlier, it is patently clear that he was a businessman first, last and all the time: finance was all-important. Hardly any reference is made to the products the company manufactured during his time – he could quite easily have gone into some other industry with equal success.

He was not an engineer and was probably not even a cyclist or motorcyclist. It was a happy coincidence for us that the great cycle boom occurred just as he arrived in England and he saw the opportunity to make money in this new and exciting business.

I had the privilege of being introduced to Mr Bettmann when he visited Meriden soon after the war. He was a short portly man, and despite having lived in England for over sixty-five years, spoke with a pronounced German accent.

If I had known then that I would be writing about him some years later, I would have enjoyed talking to him about the early days of the company, it would have been fascinating listening to the man who created Triumph.

Siegfried Bettmann – Civic Leader

The following extracts from the *Coventry Evening Telegraph* on the day Mr Bettmann died, 24 September 1951, will give some idea of the remarkable extent of the activities in which he was involved in addition to those concerned with Triumph:

Having come to Coventry Mr Bettmann began to play an increasingly important part in the administration of his adopted city and was elected a member of the City Council for the former Bishop Street Ward. He was made Mayor in 1913. As Mayor he started many charitable funds, notably the Prince of Wales's Fund which raised nearly £8,000 in its first weeks. He was also responsible for starting a fund to accommodate Belgian refugees.

He was one of the founders and a former president of the Coventry Chamber of Commerce, and was at one time a member of the Advisory Council for the Commercial and Industrial section of Birmingham University. He was also a former president of the British Cycle and Motor Cycle Manufacturers and Traders Union. He was made a Justice of the Peace for Warwickshire in 1903 and . . . sat on the Coventry County Bench. An active member of the Coventry Liberal Association . . . Mr Bettmann took part in the election campaigns of Mr A E W Mason, Mr Silas K Hocking and Mr D M Mason. He was president of the Coventry Liberal Association for many years up to 1940.

His work in the city enabled him to say with pride, as long ago as 1923: 'There are three episodes in my life which entitle me to say that I have not lived in vain: that, although a foreign importation, I have been accepted in this city as a fully-fledged citizen; that I have been Mayor of the city at a time of national emergency; and that I am the founder of an industrial undertaking which, from the smallest beginning, has developed into a position which enables a not insignificant portion of Coventry's population to earn its living.'

His charitable acts were many, and he founded the Annie Bettmann Foundation in 1920 as a tribute to his wife who died in 1941. Of her he wrote 'She was a most gracious and charitable lady, who had rendered valuable service to the Coventry Nursing Institute of which she was a life member'. In his leisure time Mr Bettmann drew upon his travels for a series of books and the countries he wrote about included Egypt, India and South Africa. He was a prominent Freemason, he was founder of St John's Lodge, Coventry and its first elected Master.

Following Mr Bettmann's death at the age of 88, on 24 September 1951, Mr C J Band, one of the trustees of his estate handed over to the Mayor, Councillor Harry Weston, the bequests left to the city by Mr Bettmann. These included nearly 2,000 books, a Sèvres vase, a portrait in oils of Mr Bettmann by Mr C D Ward, a presentation album signed by people in many parts of the world, a badge and chain presented to Mrs Annie Bettmann as a memento of her period of office as Mayoress, and an illuminated address presented to Mr Bettmann by employees of the Triumph Company.

Mr Band said he had been a personal friend of Mr Bettmann for nearly fifty years. 'He was one of the most remarkable men I have ever known. He had many admirable qualities but I only want to refer to one – his charity, which was widespread.' There were, said Mr Band, hundreds of people in Coventry who had reason to be grateful for what Mr Bettmann had done for them. He had left the Annie Bettmann Foundation which provided grants to citizens for starting a business, but he had been responsible also for many private acts of charity. Towards the end of his life he had been giving away half of his net income. That was not an easy thing for any man to do, however rich, in present day circumstances . . .

The Mayor acknowledged the gifts with thanks and said 'No man born in a foreign country could have made himself more a Coventrian. We are more than proud to find that he was with us at the end, as at the beginning'.

Claude Vivian Holbrook

Holbrook was the son of the newspaper magnate Sir Arthur Holbrook. He has been described as 'a pleasant business man well liked by everyone in the Triumph organization'. He was knighted in 1938, but the car company was in the hands of the Receiver a year later and was acquired by the Standard Motor Company. Holbrook served again in World War II and as Colonel Sir Claude Vivian Holbrook was at various times Deputy Lieutenant of Warwickshire, a magistrate and a county councillor. He died in 1979 at the age of ninety-three.

Claude Vivian Holbrook, who joined Triumph after World War I as Works Manager.

Claude Vivian Holbrook (1886–1979)

In Mr Bettmann's own story he recounts how he came to meet Colonel Holbrook who was at the War Office handling the procurement of motorcycles for the forces in 1914, when World War I started. Bettmann was so impressed with Holbrook that after the war he invited him to join the Triumph company as Works Manager, replacing Schulte with whom he had fallen out.

Holbrook was very keen to get Triumph into the car industry and wanted a small car to compete with the celebrated Austin Seven. A big design team was built up headed by A A Sykes, Chief Draughtsman and Walter Belgrove, a distinguished body designer. The result of their efforts was the Triumph Super Seven, selling at under £200, and it achieved considerable success. In 1930 Holbrook was promoted to Assistant Managing Director and replaced Bettmann as Managing Director three years later.

Holbrook was not enthusiastic about the successful Super Seven and wanted something more impressive (Bettmann's own story confirms Holbrook's constant desire for change).

The depression of the early thirties had a disastrous effect on Triumph, as on most other companies in the Coventry area and elsewhere. A decision was made to cease motorcycle production and concentrate on cars. By 1935 Triumph had stopped building small cars (8 and 10hp) to concentrate on the bigger Gloria in another Coventry factory in the Foleshill Road which had been acquired by Holbrook. The motorcycle business was sold to Jack Sangster of Ariel, in whose hands it was transformed into an enormously successful business.

Triumph cars and motorcycles had now parted company for good.

Mauritz Johann Schulte

Schulte was an engineer, a German from Nuremberg like Bettmann, whom he joined in 1887. He organized the move from London to Coventry in order to get into manufacturing and located and set up the plant off Much Park Street in the centre of the city.

'Ixion' (the Rev B H Davies), that famous contributor to *The Motor Cycle* for so many years and who knew Schulte well, said that in his opinion, the sport and business concerned with motorcycles was saved from extinction at the time by two things: 1. The invention of the Simms–Bosch high tension magneto, and 2. The intervention of M J Schulte, a man of 'great vigour, of cool and balanced judgement and of considerable prudence'. That was some testimonial!

Schulte was responsible for the production of the first Triumph motorcycles which appeared in 1902, details of which will be found on page 24.

From the primitive 1902 model with its 2¼hp Minerva engine slung under the front down tube, direct belt drive and full pedalling gear, Schulte progressed rapidly so that

Mauritz J Schulte, also from Nuremberg – a skilled engineer responsible for the high quality of Triumph products in the early days.

at the outbreak of war in 1914, Triumph could offer the 550cc Type H, which had a reliable and powerful engine, chain primary transmission to a Sturmey Archer 3-speed gearbox, strong frame and forks and controls on the handlebars – in essence, the modern motorcycle.

His products earned the title 'Trusty' and many an army despatch rider had reason to thank his Trusty Triumph for getting him through the shot and shell of the Flanders battle fronts.

Schulte served Triumph nobly from 1887 to 1919 when he retired, following some difficulties he had with Bettmann. They had been together a long time! His departure was softened by a golden handshake of £15,000 – a truly generous amount at that time.

Dirty Work in the Isle of Man!

Back in 1973 I received a letter from Mr A C Anderson of New Zealand who rode a Triumph in the 1914 Senior TT.

Charles Hathaway

In Mr Bettmann's brief history, he refers to his Works Manager Charles Hathaway. Now Mr Hathaway is virtually unknown to most people, yet he was a very influential character in the early days and had a profound effect on the fortunes of the company. He was a talented designer as well as a Works Manager and was much involved with Schulte in producing the first all-Triumph motorcycle in 1905. A later Triumph catalogue, referring to this model says: 'The large part played by Mr Hathaway in the design of this machine will always be remembered.' He also designed and patented the famous horizontal spring fork which was a unique Triumph feature for so many years. The very popular 225cc two-stroke 'Junior' model, which was included in the range from 1913 to 1925, was also his work.

It was so interesting that I kept it in my files and having recently rediscovered it, I would like to quote some extracts. At that time Mr Schulte was very much a power in the land at Triumph and of him Mr Anderson says:

I do know that he was a very wealthy man interested in many large concerns including the BSA and the North British Rubber Company . . .

For the 1914 TT the company made a great effort to win as they got the services of the man who was second in the 1913 race. We were told to 'do our best' and I beat him by four minutes so that is why Mr Schulte was pleased with me. There were two trade riders who were jealous of me for beating them so easily in the practice runs. I had worn the nuts almost off on both sides of the footrests as well as part of the centre piece and those two trade riders came to me in our garage and said that I hadn't done that on the road but had used a file. I still regret not having told Mr Schulte about that, especially as I knew that those two riders had put their bikes on the stands, set the engines going and then pressed the rear tyres against a hard surface to wear the tyres down so as to make believe they had done it on the road. When they would do an underhand thing like that, I came to the conclusion that they had 'fixed' my bike, as they could always get into our garage.

I didn't get a mile in the race when I had to replace a plug and I had no bother at all with plugs in the practising. My belt fastener also came adrift. When in the race I stopped for petrol, the attendant told me that almost certainly my bike had been interfered with and the same thing had happened in the 1913 race. As the Triumphs used North British Rubber Company tyres, I certainly should have told Mr Schulte my story.

I used a German make of tyre on the rear wheel as they had studs on the sides and I could corner better with them. I also found that the two springs in the front (the old model) was far better than the single spring and the company put the old ones on for me.

The company took the whole of 'The Prince of Wales' hotel at Ramsey. There were about thirty all told of us – including Mr and Mrs Schulte and the eldest daughter (please excuse my writing as I'm a bit shaky – some excuse as I am eighty-six). You will wonder why I am interested in Muriel Schulte, but it is a sad story for me. I stayed with the Schultes quite a few times and Muriel and I – well, love at first sight with both of us. Her mother was very nice to me and welcomed me to their home when I went back to the war in 1917. But I was mustard gassed in the war and you know what that meant and I was told by the Medical Superintendent at Brockenhurst Hospital that I would not live very long. So I thought the most honourable thing I could do was to go back to New Zealand and not see Muriel again. If I had gone and told her what I was going to do, she was such a lovely girl that she would not agree with that. Rightly or wrongly I did not want to ruin her life, but I have regretted leaving her and if she is not alive now she will have died thinking ill of me.

These extracts show that competition in the Isle of Man was just as keen before World War I as it is today.

However, destroying the tread on the tyres to prove how hard you have ridden is not, I am sure, something to which Ray Pickrell or Percy Tait would stoop!

A typical scene in those first Isle of Man TT days. The rider is J R Haswell, who finished on his Triumph in 1911 and 1912.

3

The Bettmann Motorcycles

The Bettmann era ran from 1885 to 1936 and it was in this period that the motorcycle grew up from being a crude motorized bicycle to the fairly sophisticated, high performance vehicle that we knew in pre-war days. I say 'fairly' because it does not compare with the degree of sophistication which we have seen in motorcycle design in recent times.

Nevertheless, it will be interesting to look at the Triumph products of the Bettmann era and try to pick out the significant models which led the way forward throughout this period.

No 1 – 1902 2¼hp Minerva

We start with what we always call 'No 1'. This famous model of 1902 has appeared in Triumph catalogues from time to time through the years to make the point that Triumph were real pioneers in the motorcycle industry.

It was a simple enough machine comprising a Triumph pedal cycle, which had probably been strengthened to take a 2¼hp Belgian Minerva engine mounted at the bottom of the front down tube. This drove the rear wheel from the crankshaft by means of a long belt. A Belgian engine was used because the Continentals were ahead of the UK in engine technology at the time, and Schulte wanted the best engine he could get until he was ready to produce his own.

1905 3hp Triumph

By 1905 Schulte and Hathaway had produced this machine, designed and built entirely in Coventry. The engine was a single-cylinder side-valve 78 x 76mm (363cc) for which 3hp was claimed at 1,500rpm. It was also said to be the first engine to have its mainshaft supported on ball bearings. Transmission again was by a long belt direct from the crankshaft to the rear wheel. Ignition was by accumulator, but for an extra £5 you could have a Simms-Bosch magneto, which was strongly recommended by the factory.

The first Triumph motorcycle. Produced in 1902 it had a 2¼hp Belgian Minerva engine.

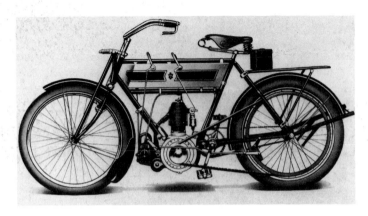

Triumph 3hp from 1906 with magneto ignition,
strongly recommended by the manufacturers, but
costing £5 extra.

1908 3½hp with Variable Pulley

In 1907 the engine measured 82 x 86mm (453cc) and in 1908 it was enlarged again to 84 x 86mm (476cc). The 1908 3½hp model was specified with a variable pulley. This provided alternative ratios at a time when hills were held in some awe. The pulley on the crankshaft screwed in and out to provide alternative ratios of 4:1 and 6:1, but necessitated a somewhat complicated roadside procedure, as the drive belt had to be shortened or lengthened by means of small detachable sections. It was a better than

nothing attempt to deal with the hill-climbing problem, but not much fun if it was raining!

1911 3½hp Free Engine Model

Triumph were not backward in trying to solve the obvious control problems of a motorcycle with a direct drive from the engine to the rear wheel. Traffic was relatively light in those days, but even so the absence of a clutch must have been embarrassing at times. So in 1911 Triumph announced the Free Engine model. This had a plate clutch embodied in the back hub and operated by heel and toe pedal. To quote the catalogue: 'This allows the rider to start from rest whilst seated in the saddle, and thus obviates running alongside and leaping into the saddle whilst the machine is in motion'. The more elderly riders must have sighed with relief! With the variable pulley and now the free engine clutch, things were improving fast. However, the sight of a Triumph, stationary but with its engine running and the rear wheel pulley revolving was an unusual one.

1911 3½hp Tourist Trophy Racer

In 1907 Jack Marshall came second in the first Isle of Man TT Race (single cylinder class), riding a 3½hp Triumph.

He won it the next year at 40.49mph (65.16kph) with the fastest lap of the race at 42.48mph (63.35kph). Sir R Arbuthnot came third on a similar model. Other Triumphs finished in fourth, fifth, seventh and tenth places, with just one retirement.

In 1910 eight Triumphs started and eight finished, a fact which is recorded in the 1911 catalogue. The TT Racer was claimed to be a facsimile of the machines ridden in the Isle of Man. It had the standard 85 x 88mm 3½hp engine of the time, with belt drive and variable pulley (high 3¼, low 4½:1). Pedalling gear was dispensed with and two sets of footrests were provided.

1915 4hp Type H

The year 1914 saw the start of the Great War and Triumph became a major supplier of motorcycles to the forces. The model pressed into service was a big step forward. This was the Type H which was equipped with a countershaft three-speed Sturmey Archer gearbox with chain primary drive. Final drive was by the inevitable belt which could not have been much of an asset in the mud of Flanders. The engine was the standard civilian 550cc (4hp) side-valve and so successful was the H that it earned the nickname 'Trusty Triumph' which stuck for years. In fact,

TT Racer, 1911. The catalogue claimed this was 'a facsimile of the Triumph Motors which figured so prominently in the last TT Race' – eight started and eight finished!

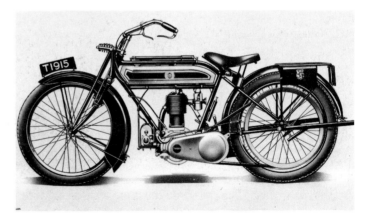

Model H, from 1915 – 550cc side-valve with Sturmey Archer three-speed gearbox. In all, some 30,000 were supplied to Allied Forces in World War I.

the telegraphic address of the company right to the very end was 'Trusty Coventry'.

1920 4hp Type SD

The end of the war also saw the end of the belt drive on the 4hp Triumph. The new model was very similar to the Model H except that it had all-chain drive. The drive, in fact, crossed over through the gearbox, the final drive being on the offside of the motorcycle. It was known as the SD which stood for 'Spring Drive' as the clutch now incorporated a transmission shock absorber.

1922 500cc OHV Type IR Fast Roadster (Riccy)

The Triumph company entered six machines for the 1921 Senior TT in the Isle of Man. The standard SD now had an engine of 550cc which was too big for this race, so obviously something different was brewing. When it appeared it caused quite a sensation. It was a 500cc single-cylinder with four overhead valves operated by pushrods – the Japanese were very late in the field with their four-valve heads. The top half of the engine had been designed by Ricardo & Co Ltd, specialists in piston and combustion chamber design – Harry Ricardo was the man responsible for the design. The valves were set at 90deg to each other, the exhaust valves discharging into two separate

The famous 1924 500cc OHV four-valve Ricardo model, nicknamed the 'Riccy'. It broke many world speed records in the twenties.

pipes, the inlet valves being fed by a single carburettor tract.

The results in the race were very disappointing: only one machine finished, and that was in sixteenth place. Nevertheless, extensive development went on and ultimately the 'Riccy' as it was called, collected a large number of world records in the very capable hands of Frank Halford, who later became a distinguished aircraft designer and then Managing Director of the De Havilland Engine Co. It took the flying mile at 83.91mph (135.01kph), the one hour at 76.74mph (123.47kph) and the fifty miles at 77.27mph (124.33kph). Harry Ricardo was later knighted for his services to the motor industry.

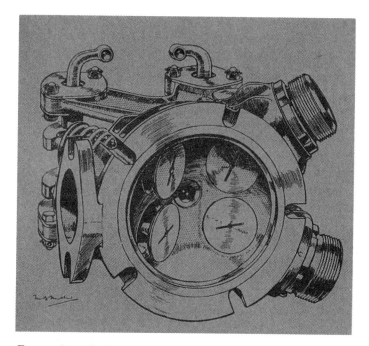

Four-valve cylinder head designed by Sir Harry Ricardo; it was ahead of its time.

In the 1922 Senior TT, Walter Brandish finished a very creditable second at 56.52mph (90.95kph). The Riccy featured in the Triumph range for the next five years and was discontinued in 1927 when its place at the top of the range was taken by an entirely new all-Triumph 500cc OHV, the Type TT.

1924 494cc Type P

The twenties were not a flourishing time for the Triumph company and something had to be done to keep the big Priory Street works turning over profitably. The story goes that Bettmann asked the drawing office for a really basic 500 which could be produced quickly in large numbers and sold at the lowest possible price – and so would return a profit of some kind.

The result was the famous (or infamous) Model P 494cc side-valve. It was simple enough and employed a number of rather dubious cost-cutting design features which eventually backfired on the company. The first build was 20,000 machines and the price was a closely guarded secret until the machine was actually on display at the 1924 London Show.

The price ticket read £42.17s.6d, which delighted the public and demoralized the competition. The excitement can be appreciated when you realize that the SD at that time was priced at £83.

Orders poured in and the works were so stretched that they, on occasion, produced 1,000 machines in a week – which was just cause for celebration. However, there was not much celebration when the P reached the customers. Complaints concerned the front brake (a loop of asbestos string round a small pulley), the clutch operation, the big-end bearing and many other things. Nothing could be done by way of rectification on the first 20,000, but the Mark II was reworked and eventually did something to restore the reputation of this unfortunate model.

The famous (or infamous!) 1924 model P, 494cc side-valve which went on sale for £42.17s.6d., causing great alarm among other manufacturers.

Two Strangers

Throughout the Bettmann era, Triumph design followed a steady and not very adventurous path: the products were good, honest motorcycles of their day; they were reliable, well made and reasonably priced. However, on two occasions, the design office must have had a rush of blood to the head and produced models which, apart from the colour of the tanks, bore little or no resemblance to what had gone before.

1913 225cc Junior

The Junior was a 225cc two-stroke with a countershaft 2-speed gear but no clutch. The gearbox was chain driven and final drive was the good old belt, so beloved by Triumph designers. The gears were controlled by a cable from a handlebar lever, the rider engaging low gear and paddling off to start the engine. Although the company called it the Junior, the public insisted on 'Baby Triumph' and that name persisted.

One of these turned up at Meriden years ago (it was *en route* to the USA, I believe) and I rode it round the sports field. It was a delightful little beast once you had mastered the clutchless operation. Oddly enough, America took a fancy to this bike and Ignatz Schwinn of Chicago (who made the big Excelsior twin and Henderson Four) was licensed to produce it, stepped up to 269cc. It did not last long, but the famous Triumph horizontal spring fork was still being used on Schwinn bicycles in the seventies!

A unique Triumph feature in the early days was this rocking spring fork. Hinged at the base of the steering head, movement was controlled by a horizontal spring at the top. It worked quite well at the limited speeds of the time.

1924 346cc Type LS

The other 'odd ball' was the LS. This was a 350 side-valve single with a three-speed gearbox built in unit with the

Sir Harry Ralph Ricardo. His work on engines made a significant contribution to the success of the car industry in its early years.

Sir Harry Ralph Ricardo (1885–1974)

Ricardo was a distinguished consulting engineer specializing in power units. His work on the almost universally used side-valve engine in British cars between the wars was widely recognized. In his early days, he worked on aircraft engines as well as cars so that the 4-valve OHV Triumph nicknamed after him, the 'Riccy', brought motorcycle engines into his orbit as well. He became a Fellow of the Royal Society in 1929 and was knighted in 1948.

engine. It had a gear primary drive, all metal (steel and copper) clutch, and mechanical force-feed lubrication. This almost 'space age' spec was let down by the fact that the rear brake was a dummy belt rim – although when originally announced, it had drum brakes on both wheels. It was a long way ahead of its time and this possibly deterred the customers, for it soon disappeared from the range.

1929 498cc Type ST

The Riccy seemed to fall out of favour with the management in its later years, and was eventually replaced by the

Model ST, 1929. A very advanced twin-port OHV single-cylinder with enclosed, lubricated valve-gear and roller-bearing rockers.

two-valve Model TT as was mentioned earlier. This engine was developed by Victor Horsman, the famous Brooklands rider-tuner (and later Liverpool dealer).

The TT was an impressive looking machine with its two-port OHV head and enclosed valve gear with roller bearing rockers. The three-speed gearbox had a crossover drive as used in earlier side-valve models. The new type forks had large adjustable fabric-friction discs and a steering damper was included. Brakes were internal expanding front and rear. Later, in 1929, it became the ST as illustrated on the previous page.

Pre-Turner Twins

There were two vertical (or parallel) twins in the Triumph story before Turner introduced his immortal Speed Twin. The first was in 1913 and did not get beyond the prototype stage. The other was Val Page's 1932 6/1.

The 1913 twin, designed by Schulte and Hathaway, was a 600cc side-valve with a horizontally-split crankcase, like a car engine. The 180deg crankshaft, a one-piece forging, was supported on widely spaced double-row ball main bearings. The left-hand end of the shaft carried a forged-steel outside flywheel. The camshaft, on ball races, was at right angles to the crankshaft and was driven by a large skew gear, machined on the centre web of the crankshaft. Cams were at each end of the shaft and operated the valves through adjustable tappets. The magneto was driven by another skew gear at the end of the camshaft. The

An early example of a vertical twin engine, produced experimentally by Triumph in 1913. It had side-valves, a horizontally-split, car-type crankcase and an outside flywheel.

pistons rose and fell alternately, unlike the other two Triumph twins. Nothing came of this engine; maybe World War I put a stop to it, although rumour has it that vibration was a problem. It was still a problem in modern times – particularly in the 750cc-plus categories in which some makers indulged. Edward Turner always reckoned that 650cc was the largest satisfactory capacity for a vertical twin and he never went above it, nor did Val Page.

Tribute to Bob Currie

This photograph came into my possession some years ago and I cannot remember who gave it to me. The fact that it was taken outside the Triumph Works (*see* signboard) made it of more than usual interest. I sent it to Bob Currie, whose death in July 1988 came as a great shock to all his friends, and asked him whether he could tell me anything about it. Bob was editor of *Classic Motor Cycle* and knew more about the vintage and veteran side of motorcycling than any other six persons put together, in my opinion. He wrote back:

The late Bob Currie's analysis of this old photograph makes absorbing reading. Why do they all look so serious? There's hardly a smile to be seen anywhere!

I'm afraid I still haven't been able to identify the occasion, but the date is early 1921, for the following reasons:

1. The outfit in the immediate foreground has the enclosed-type horizontal fork spring, new for the 1921 season, and is therefore the all-chain-drive Model SD. The other outfit, with light coloured Triumph Gloria sidecar, has the bridged but exposed fork spring and is a Model H, as also is the solo on the right of the shot, just ahead of the round-tank 225cc Junior.
2. Tax discs were introduced late in 1921, but none are visible on any of the machines, so it must be before tax discs became compulsory. On the other hand, Magdyno electric lighting was offered for 1921 on the Model H and Model SD for the first time, at extra cost (both outfits have electric headlamps).
3. National Benzole increased their price to 4/- a gallon in March 1921, and this could be some sort of publicity effort to counter sales resistance by road users. [Bob does not mention that the signs on the sidecars read, with a magnifying glass!, '5000 miles National Benzole Test'.]

How's that for a masterly piece of detective work, typical of Bob? One other interesting feature of this photograph is that I am fairly sure that the two gentlemen standing on the extreme left are none other than Siegfried Bettmann and Col. Claude V Holbrook.

And how about the amazing array of very large 'flat hats' which were obviously *de rigueur* for the dedicated motorcyclist in those days. They were not, however, the famous 'Coventry Caps' which had seven panels and a button on top and which can still be seen around in the city today.

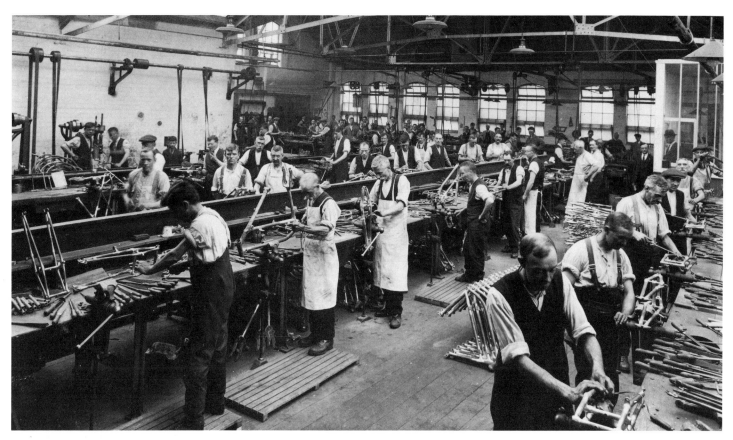

An interesting shot taken in the old Triumph Priory Street Works. This was the Frame Shop and every man is at his bench and working hard (for the benefit of the photographer no doubt).

Model CN, 1929, 498cc. Moving into modern times with a neat saddle tank. The cradle frame and large brakes were major departures from the 'vintage' look of earlier models.

Val Page's 1932 twin, (*see also* page 39), did get into production, but it was not very popular. It was a good sidecar puller and in 1933 won the Maudes Trophy by covering 500 miles (800km) in under 500 minutes at Brooklands, with sidecar attached. It nearly achieved further fame the following year, when an under-bored 500cc supercharged version was built in an attempt to win the trophy offered by *The Motor Cycle* for the first British multi to cover 100 miles (160km) in the hour. Ridden by TT rider Tommy Spann, it put in some promising initial laps of the Brooklands circuit at around the 150mph (170kph) mark when it ran into magneto trouble and finished up on one cylinder.

Unfortunately on the same day (Wednesday 1 August) the New Imperial concern were at the track in full force with their 500cc V-twin, with Ginger Wood in the saddle and after and uneventful run, claimed the trophy at 102.21mph (164.48kph).

Flat Tanks Out!

Before the Bettmann era came to an end and to combat the slump which was beginning to bite, an effort was made to bring the models up to date and make them more attractive by replacing the traditional flat tank (a Triumph feature since the very early days) with a shapely saddle tank. Most manufacturers were doing the same at this time; it was a fashion, like sloping engines. However, it was a fashion which has lasted to the present time. The model CN demonstrates the much improved appearance.

4

The Modern Era

Enter Val Page

Triumph can be said to have moved out of the vintage era with the appointment in 1932 of Val Page, one of the most competent designers our industry has known. Page came from Ariel, who were going through a rough patch, and Triumph were lucky to get him. Before Ariel, he had been with J A Prestwich & Co Ltd (JAP) of Tottenham, the well-known engine manufacturers, where he eventually became Chief Designer. There, he designed a 250 which would run at 8,000rpm (unprecedented in the twenties) and he also designed the engines used in the Brough Superior SS100 and SS80 models as well as many others.

On arrival at Triumph, he set about producing a completely new range of models which comprised 250, 350 and 500cc OHV singles, 350 and 550cc side-valve singles and a 650cc OHV vertical twin. They were a first class, well designed and well made collection of motorcycles. So good were they that some of them, suitably modified, served as the basis of the range offered by the Triumph Engineering Co Ltd when they took over in 1936.

1935 250cc 2/5

Val Page insisted on a high degree of commonality in his specifications and the 250, 350 and 500cc models looked

This is the Model 2/5 250cc which cost £53.

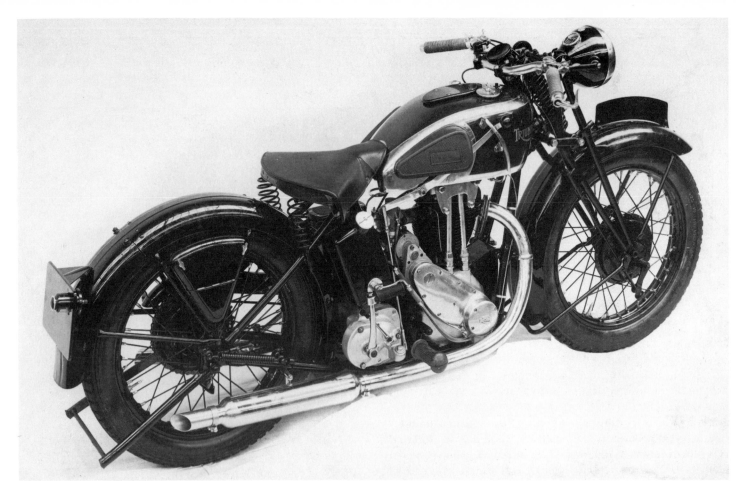

Another Page model in the same league. This is the 1935 5/2 500cc OHV twin-port with four speeds, Magdyno lighting, electric horn, etc., which the catalogue described as: 'A fast, full-sized machine for solo or sidecar.'

very similar to each other, which made the smaller models look a little overweight. The 2/1 had a 63 x 80mm (249cc) engine with totally enclosed and lubricated valve gear, and a four-speed gearbox which had at last found its way into the Triumph range. Note that the bore and stroke is the same as that of the Triumph 500cc twins which came along much later. Selling at £53, the model also included a saddle tank, twin-port head and Magdyno lighting.

1935 500cc 5/2

There were three 500cc models in this group, the 5/2, 5/5 and 5/10. The first two were virtually identical but the 5/10 was a racer pure and simple. All had four-speed gear-boxes and deep saddle tanks. Tankside gearchange was standard, but foot control cost £1 extra.

1935 650cc 6/1

Here was something completely different: a vertical twin, long before the modern versions came out. The 6/1 was a 360deg twin with a single camshaft at the rear of the block operating the valves by unequal length pushrods working in a tunnel cast in the block – a similar arrangement to that used by BSA and Norton after the war. The primary drive was by helical gears without an intermediate gear so that the engine ran 'backwards'. The four-speed gearbox was bolted solidly to the rear of the engine. It was primarily a sidecar puller and was reputed to be 'unburstable'.

Troubled Times – And the Rescue

Despite the new range of Val Page models, the company was not doing well at this time (due in part to overstretching itself on the car side). In a time of depression they

The 6/1. A vertical twin long before Edward Turner's famous Speed Twin. 650cc, OHV, four-speed unit construction gearbox, 8in brakes; this was a 'real man's' motorcycle. Costing £77, sadly, it did not sell in large numbers. Ahead of its time maybe?

made the astonishing decision to go into production with the very expensive 2.3-litre straight-eight Triumph Gloria Dolomite. This was a Coventry-built version of the Alfa Romeo 8C (winner of the 1931 Le Mans 24-hour race, driven by Lord Howe and Tim Birkin). The Alfa company would have the Italian rights to make the Triumph 6/1 vertical twin motorcycle engine, but nothing came of this project in the end.

The car did not get very far either; only three were made in the Priory Street toolroom.

Things went from bad to worse and the decision was made to finish with motorcycles altogether and concentrate on the car side in a newly acquired factory in the Holbrooks area of Coventry.

It was at this point that Jack Sangster came into the picture. He had rescued the ailing Ariel company in 1932, and restored its fortunes, and when he heard that the motorcycle side of Triumph was being offered for sale, he moved in. He bought the nominal capital of the Triumph Engineering Co Ltd, a non-trading subsidiary of the Triumph Company which had been registered on 23 April 1906 with an initial capital of £100. This was increased to £21,000 on 25 February 1936. The new company then took over most of the Priory Street works, together with the motorcycle plant and machinery, and as from 22 January 1936, the cars and motorcycles parted company forever. The bicycles had been disposed of some time before.

Details of the purchase make interesting reading today:

	£ s d
Goodwill, patents, trade marks, and registered designs	600.00.0
Buildings and premises	20,000.00.0
Fixtures, fittings and office furniture	400.00.0
Plant and machinery	28,586.05.6
	49,586.05.6
From this was deducted the amount realized by the sale of scrap metal, scrap timber, obsolete tools and machinery:	8,055.10.5
So, ignoring a number of minor transactions we finish up with a total of:	41,530.10.5

A bargain! No wonder that Edward Turner in his letter to me (*see* page 43) said, 'I induced Mr Sangster to buy the Triumph name. This was purchased at a very low figure.'

Bettmann – Chairman!

It was at this point that Sangster invited Bettmann to be Chairman of the new company. Bettmann mentions this at the end of his story (*see* Chapter 1) and one imagines that he was very pleased to accept, as he could perhaps see that his precious Triumph company, the company that he had started half a century earlier, was now going into safe hands and would perhaps prosper again – he would have been staggered to know just how much!

John Young Sangster

I met JS many times during my years at Meriden. He was always courteous, friendly, ready to discuss whatever was going on in the business at the time and he never forgot your name.

One of his most difficult jobs must have been the occasion when, in 1951, he told the assembled senior staff at Meriden that he had sold Triumph to BSA – you could have heard a pin drop! Full details of this sale can be found later on in Chapter 13.

Mr Sangster was meticulous in everything he did. I used to supply his personal stationery and the dimensions of the sheets had to be exact to a 'thou' or the order was rejected. He had some odd little quirks too – although a millionaire, I have known him send the chain from his domestic bath plug all the way from London to the works to be chrome plated! On the other hand, for many years all managers at Meriden used to receive a chicken and a substantial joint of meat at Christmas, with a label of good wishes signed personally by Sangster, a much appreciated gesture.

Following his death, a memorial service was held at the Grosvenor Chapel, London, on 19 April 1977. This was very

John Young Sangster, the man who rescued Triumph from oblivion in 1936 and saw it become so successful that he sold it for £2½m fifteen years later.

well attended by members of the company and industry and the address was given by Mr Eric Turner, Chairman of the BSA Group.

This appointment was a very shrewd one on Sangster's part, as Bettmann's reputation with the suppliers and dealers both at home and overseas was very high. It was a short-term appointment only, but long enough for him to realize that things were going to go well. Go well they did too, as the story continues into those fateful few years before war broke out again in Europe. One wonders what Siegfried Bettmann's feelings were when his erstwhile homeland plunged the world into yet another titanic struggle – which also brought about the complete destruction of the great Priory Street factory, his workplace for over thirty years.

TWN (Triumph Werke Nuremberg)

Perhaps it should be mentioned here that Triumph in Coventry had an associated company in Nuremberg, Germany. This is not surprising when the German origin of our company is considered. The two worked together from 1903 and the motorcycles they produced had a family likeness for some time. However this had ceased by 1929 and although TWN continued to make motorcycles until 1957, they eventually moved to typewriters which then carried the familiar Triumph logo.

John Young Sangster
(1896–1977)

John Young Sangster (or 'JS' as he was known at Triumph) was born in 1896, the son of a mechanical engineer of Scottish descent. His father was Director and General Manager of a cycle firm which acquired the Ariel company – Ariel made motorcycles, motor tricycles and cars. JS

served in the army in the Great War and on his return, designed a two-cylinder car which the Rover company took up as the Rover 8. Sangster was given the job of organizing production, which he did very efficiently.

He left Rover to become Assistant Managing Director to his father in Components Ltd in 1922, but the Ariel Nine and Ten cars were not successful against the mass-produced Austin and Morris and production ended in 1925. Val Page joined Ariel at this time and set about designing a new range of motorcycles.

In 1929 Edward Turner also came to Selly Oak, and the famous Turner/Sangster partnership started, although the significance of this could not have been appreciated at the time. The year 1929 brought the great depression and Ariel struggled on until 1932, when they were forced into liquidation. Sangster was able to buy the machinery and part of the premises and began trading as Ariel Motors (JS) Ltd. Thanks largely to Turner's work, the Ariel range began to offer some highly saleable products and the company prospered. So much so that when Triumph were looking for a buyer for their motorcycle company in 1936, they had to look no further than John Young Sangster.

5

The Rise of Triumph

When I first thought of writing a book about Triumph, the obvious subject was a history of the company. I therefore approached Edward Turner for his blessing on the project. This would give me access to the company archives and the use of any photographs and other material held in my own department. The BSA/Triumph Group was in desperate trouble at this time, so I think readers will find the extracts from his reply to me very interesting in view of what happened subsequently. The history was never written, but the book that did emerge, *It's a Triumph*, was basically historical.

Capel, Surrey
10 July 1973

My dear Davies,

Thank you for your letter and enclosures which I read with some interest . . . I have been following the Norton-Villiers proposed amalgamation with BSA/Triumph and have agreed that the block of shares I still retained out of loyalty to the old company be converted to NVT as it appeared to me that it was this or a Receiver stepping in to take over BSA/Triumph, in which case everyone there would be out of a job. After the awful mess made by Eric Turner, Sturgeon and Jofeh of a good motorcycle business, I do hope Dennis Poore realizes what he is getting into, but certainly I wish him well.

With regard to your history of Triumph, to create an authoritative history of this old company is quite a job, particularly if it is going to be interesting. You will have to go back to a Jewish gentleman named Bettmann, who came over from Nuremberg to the cycle city of Coventry to make bicycles and he brought with him some German engineers, in particular a man called Schulte and a cost clerk named Schwemmer. They went into motorcycle manufacture with an imported engine until Schulte designed a 500cc side-valve motor which worked and afterwards became a 550cc which was the power unit used in the famous model in World War I.

History then goes on, up to the time when Colonel Holbrook became Managing Director, which arose from a friendship with Bettmann, who used to see him at the War Office for contracts for motorcycles in 1914. Sir Claude, as he now is, if he is still alive, was from the start more interested in cars and quickly depleted the resources of a sound company in numerous experiments on motor cars, culminating with the Dolomite with which Donald Healey had a great deal to do. By this time in the twenties and early thirties the motorcycle business went to pot.

Edward Turner, the man who made Triumph so successful with his brilliantly-conceived designs and economical management. His vertical twin engine, in various sizes, powered a range of motorcycles for over forty years.

After Ariel went broke, several Ariel people, like Harry Perrey and Val Page joined Triumph and got them going on a more sound motorcycle, which was heavy and rather expensive and not particularly saleable. It was then decided by the Parent Board to cease manufacture of motorcycles entirely. My old Ariel friends, with whom I had occasional contact, informed me what was going on and at this time I felt that I had reached the end of my useful career with Ariel and induced Mr Sangster to buy the Triumph name. This was purchased at a very low figure, leasing the plant, factory and agreeing to sell the spares stock on commission, and this was the birth of Triumph Engineering, one of the old company names never used, but which was restored to differentiate the two Triumph companies. From thereon plenty of people left today can tell you what went on in the company under my direction up to the time when you joined it after the war.

I shall be interested in what sort of story you write in the future and will be pleased to help in any way possible.

Yours sincerely

E.T.

Edward and Siegfried

Edward Turner's letter, written barely a month before he died, gives quite an accurate account of Triumph history, so he must have studied it at some time. I expect he had read Mr Bettmann's own story or even discussed it with Mr Bettmann himself.

I would have enjoyed listening to that conversation – you can imagine the two men, who between them controlled nearly ninety years of Triumph history, sitting in front of a blazing log fire with a bottle on the table between them . . . It might have gone something like this:

ET   Tell me Siegfried, why did you come to England?

SB   England was the place to make money in those days. It had an Empire covering a quarter of the globe with endless opportunities for business. The English were enterprising and adventurous, they were good to work with.

ET   You were not an engineer yet you chose to make bicycles, how did that come about?

SB   Bicycles were booming. Once the ridiculous penny farthing was out of the way, the safety bicycle promised cheap, easy transport for the millions – and they wanted it! Horses went out of fashion! Schulte was my engineer and a very excellent one too.

ET   So I believe.

SB   You didn't do so badly either, you took over my company when it was bankrupt and turned it into a money spinner.

ET   It was not easy, but we had some good people and the product was right.

SB   I'm told it was a vertical twin – what is a vertical twin?

ET   I'll have to explain that some other time, will you have another drink?

SB   Ja, dankeschön, Herr Turner.

Enough of this fantasizing, what can be said about Edward Turner? His career has been described in several books, so we will just recap briefly here for the benefit of those not familiar with it. He was born in London, in 1901, where his father ran a light engineering company. This introduced him to the elements of the business to which he turned later on.

World War I saw him a wireless operator in the Merchant Navy. The war over, he began to take an interest in motorcycles. He was encouraged in this way by his elder brother, the owner of a quick Harley. His enthusiasm mounting, he bought a corner shop in south-east London (Peckham) and set himself up as a motorcycle dealer and repairer. He secured the Velocette franchise, and before long he was designing a motorcycle himself – not only designing, but making parts for it with the help of some basic machine tools.

Turner off duty! Presenting the prizes at the company's sports day which was held at the back of the works at Meriden.

This was a 350 face-cam single and it must have worked well because he soon started looking around for someone to produce it in quantity. There was only one place to go – the Midlands. There, he met up with J Y Sangster, and this was indeed a fortunate meeting, not only for the two men concerned but also for the British motorcycle industry which developed as a result of their combined skill and enterprise.

This was in 1929. Sangster set Turner to work in the Ariel drawing office under Val Page and with Bert Hopwood alongside. What a trio! In the years that followed, their creative abilities transformed the product range not only of Ariel but Triumph, BSA and Norton. They moved from company to company like a game of designer musical chairs. The motorcycles they designed became classics: BSA's Gold Star and Golden Flash, Norton's Dominator, Triumph's Speed Twin, Ariel's Square Four, and many more.

Back to Turner. He was the man responsible for the remarkable Ariel Square Four which was announced in 1930 and continued in production, with several facelifts, until 1952. Turner was at Ariel until 1936, taking over as Chief Designer in 1932 when Val Page went to Triumph. In 1936 Triumph were in deep trouble; Sangster moved in, took over the motorcycle side and the Priory Street works and named Edward Turner as Chief Designer and General Manager. This came as a surprise to the industry: no one doubted his abilities as a designer, but whether he could 'manage', time alone would tell.

Edward Turner at Work

So what was Edward Turner like on a day-to-day basis?

Thousands of words have been written on this subject by writers with very little experience of the gentleman in question. They may have met him, talked to him, but not worked for him. Most of their comments are based on hearsay and they condemn him out of hand as an impossible tyrant. He was very unpredictable, certainly, and when upset could be very frank! This was a side that outsiders rarely saw. In fact, our American colleagues found it difficult to believe us when we recounted some of our adventures in the great man's company! Against this, when in a good mood he had tremendous charm and this was the side the Americans always saw, for some reason.

With us, he could be very very difficult, his temper had a very short fuse, and when he blew up, you just had to stand back and take it. It can be said in his favour that these storms did not last very long, and half an hour later all was sweetness and light!

His long-suffering but impregnable secretary, the late Nan Plant, had a rough time but she did not seem to mind too much and was not averse to answering back on occasion. She acted as our 'thermometer', checking the temperature of Turner's mood of the moment and would say, when you asked to see him, 'Leave it till the morning' or, 'Come back after lunch', if the portents were not good.

There was usually a reason why he was upset. His instructions had not been followed exactly, or the job was going to cost far more than he thought it should. It was the wrong colour or the wrong shape, or maybe you had taken liberties with the project in the hope of improving it – so you took what was coming and returned next day having made sure to put things right, at which he would grunt and make no comment: just hand it back to you.

The odd thing was that despite the problems presented by his strange character, he inspired tremendous loyalty and the senior management changed very little during the whole of the thirty years I worked for Triumph. There was an unspoken feeling that Turner knew what he was doing, the company was operating very successfully and it was good to be a part of it. We were not very well paid, but that did not seem to matter, we enjoyed our work, which was more important.

Edward Turner did not have a very happy personal life as far as could be told. His first wife was killed in a car crash near Coventry in 1939. He married again many years later and although this marriage had its problems, it did produce three children, one boy and two girls, of whom ET was enormously proud.

Nan Plant, Edward Turner's secretary. Another sports day shot. She is standing next to Eric Headlam, the London and south of England sales representative.

First Moves

Once installed at Priory Street, Turner soon got to work both as a designer and a manager. Following his Ariel precedent with the Red Hunters, he took Val Page's single-cylinder models, the 2/1, 3/2 and 5/5 and with some deft touches (a silver and chrome finish and some dashing names), converted them overnight into showroom successes as the Tiger 70, 80 and 90. On the managerial side, he abolished the Sales Manager title, divided the country into three areas and appointed a manager for each. The selling

The pre-war Tiger 80 – a 350 which Turner created from Val Page's 3/2. This model, together with the other Tigers, the 250 '70' and the 500 '90' initiated the resurgence of Triumph in the market after Turner took over.

Alec Masters

Alec Masters was Service Manager. I am always grateful to Alec as he introduced me to a young lady named Doreen, who worked in his department from about 1942 onwards and who later became my wife. We subsequently covered many thousands of miles together on various Speed Twins and Thunderbirds, both solo and sidecar.

Alec was a very enthusiastic motorcyclist who rode to work daily which gave him more knowledge of the product than the customer usually had. He could therefore answer their queries and problems from his own lengthy experience on the road. During the war he served in the local Home Guard with the rank of Major.

Alec St John Masters, Service Manager at Meriden, who rode a motorcycle daily in all weathers – he knew all the answers.

operation would henceforth be conducted in the field and not from some cosy remote office in Priory Street.

But the best was still to come. Incredibly, with all the activity involved in getting the Priory Street works back into a profitable operation, Turner still found time to produce a motorcycle that altered the whole course of motorcycle design worldwide. This, of course, was the Speed Twin which was announced in July 1937. It was displayed for the first time at the London Show and caused a sensation. It bore no resemblance whatever to Val Page's 650 twin (6/1), apart from the fact that it had two parallel cylinders and a 360deg crank (the pistons went up and down together). It was its very ordinariness that was its strength. The customers were very conservative in those days and shunned anything that looked 'funny'. Many ingenious designers found this out to their cost – think of the Ascot Pullin, the P & M Panthette and the Wooller, and you will see what I mean.

The Speed Twin engine was, if anything, smaller than the Tiger 90 single and when fitted into the latter's chassis it came out 5lb (2kg) lighter than the single! Its performance was sensational; it would top 90mph (145kph) and once the tuning boys got busy 100mph- (160kph-)plus was no problem. Priced at £75, it was strictly competitive (the Tiger 90 sold at £70) and the public soon realized this. Orders poured in from the dealers and the works were hard-pressed – recalling the old days of the notorious

Alf Camwell

Alf Camwell was a valued member of Turner's team. Alf had been with Triumph for a very long time, just how long I have never been able to find out. In the 1926 catalogue there is a whole page devoted to portraits, over the heading 'Some of the Staff'. Alf Camwell features there as Machine Shop Superintendent. He later became Works Manager and after the war, in Turner's time, he joined the Board as Works Director. He had a very pleasant personality, quiet but very decisive and with a good sense of humour. He was a dyed-in-the-wool Coventrian, one of his favourite sayings being that '. . . the only good thing that ever came out of Birmingham was the Coventry Road.' No doubt a Birmingham supplier must have let him down the day he coined this remark.

Model P. It was greatly to their credit that they got into production so quickly and the fortunes of the company took a decided turn for the better.

The Works Manager responsible at this time for getting things going so effectively was Alf Camwell. As well as getting new motorcycles into production, he also had the job of closing down the car side and getting it out of the way. After the war, he became Works Director – a well deserved promotion.

6

The Speed Twin

During my thirty-odd years with Triumph, I wrote much promotion material and 'launched' many new models – the 3T de Luxe, Grand Prix, Trophy, Thunderbird, T110, Bonnie, Tina, Tigress Scooter, Trident, Ariel 3, (oh no! Not that) not forgetting the Daimler SP250 sports car. In most cases, we tried to create a real impact, with events such as the Montlhéry demo for the Thunderbird and the world speed record for the Bonnie.

Now, looking back over half a century at the introduction of the most epoch-making motorcycle of them all – the Speed Twin – it would appear that the bike, all on its own, was left to make the impact. Even in the company catalogue, all the attention it received was the following few words sandwiched in the middle of the introductory copy:

In addition, a new model is presented – the Triumph 'Speed Twin'. Founded on well tried Triumph practice, this machine incorporates an entirely new 500cc OHV vertical Twin Cylinder power unit which marks a milestone in motor cycle progress and combines a startling performance with extreme docility and silence.

That's all! Just forty-eight words to announce a model '. . . which marks a milestone in motor cycle progress'. Little did they realize how true that sentence was going to prove. What surprises me is that this modest, almost apologetic, launch of a truly sensational new model was done under the direction of Edward Turner himself. Knowing him as I do, I would have thought that he would have dreamed up some really good scheme worthy of the model itself – without spending a lot of money of course; he always watched every penny, and as the company was not two years old at that time, I doubt if there was much spare cash in the bank.

Two years later an effort was made, and the Maudes Trophy was won with an observed run by a Speed Twin and a Tiger 100 (which had been announced by then) from Land's End to John o' Groat's, plus some fast work at Brooklands. This was probably done just to consolidate the reputation built up by the twin in the market place since its introduction.

There is never any point in spending a lot of money on publicity if the product is selling well and this certainly was

The 1938 Speed Twin which altered the course of motorcycle engineering worldwide.
Turner's engine was a masterpiece of compact power. It almost killed the big single which had
reigned supreme for so many years.

Frank Baker and Henry Vale

These two contributed more than their fair share to the general well-being of the company. Both were real experts in the preparation of motorcycles, for whatever purpose they were required. Frank could breathe on an engine and it would go faster than was ever intended. He was also a master at solving knotty little mechanical problems that arose from time to time – like devising a satisfactory way to transfer the gearchange from one side of the bike to the other as required by US law. He worked in an area of the factory known to all and sundry as 'Baker's Corner'.

Henry Vale joined the Repair Shop at Priory Street in 1931. After the war he was responsible for the preparation of the works competition bikes. He was no mean performer in trials himself, so knew what was required for trials, scrambles and six-day events like the Scottish and the International Six Days Trial (ISDT). In this latter event Triumph had an unsurpassed record. Our riders were consistently chosen for the successful British Trophy and Vase teams. Some years later Vale was seconded to BSA in Birmto iron out any problems that might arise when the three-cylinder engines for the Trident and Rocket 3 went into quantity production.

the case at this time: the works were very hard pressed. This must be the explanation behind the very 'soft sell' applied to the Speed Twin. It also proves that the first and foremost requirement to run a successful business is a good product. Nothing else will do.

The opposite page reveals what the catalogue of the day says about this machine when it was first offered for sale. It was probably written by Edward Turner because it is the exact format that I had to follow in all the catalogues that I produced at Meriden for him after the war.

The Speed Twin on the Road

Before the war I had a Tiger 80 competition model which I rode regularly in South-Eastern Centre trials and some Motorcycling Club (MCC) long-distance events. It was a very good bike, it handled well and gave no trouble. I was not a very successful trials rider, but had a lot of fun.

When the war started trials finished, so I exchanged the Tiger 80 for a Speed Twin. I was in the army right from the start, in a London based anti-aircraft Signals unit, so could use a bike for nipping home to south London when I was not on duty. I found a good second-hand 1938 six-stud Speed Twin and said goodbye, rather sadly, to my Tiger. After the single-cylinder 80 with its trials gears, the Speed Twin felt like a Ferrari, it was a real flyer. I had not owned a twin before and it was quite a new experience. The easy starting, the flashing acceleration, the absence of noise, made this machine highly desirable and everyone who rode it wanted one. The success of the Speed Twin was explained . . .

When I joined Triumph after the war I had covered a lot of miles on the twin so was familiar with the product I was hired to promote, which was a great help. Soon after

1938 Speed Twin – Specification

Engine   63 x 80mm 498cc OHV double high camshaft, vertical twin. Crankshaft mounted on massive ball bearings with central flywheel. Forced feed lubrication to big ends and valve gear. Oil gauge in instrument panel. All gear drive to camshafts and Magdyno. Totally enclosed valves with accessible tappet adjustment. Connecting rods 'H' section in RR 56 Hiduminium alloy. Split big end bearings with steel caps lined with white metal.

Crankcase   High tensile aluminium alloy, heavily webbed and of great rigidity.

Crankshaft   Built up construction with centrally disposed flywheel.

Connecting Rods   'H' section in RR 56 Hiduminium alloy. Split big-end bearings with steel caps lined with white metal.

Valve Springs   Duplex Aero quality.

Carburettor   Large bore Amal. Latest Triumph Special quick-action twist grip control (patent applied for).

Petrol Tank   All-steel welded, combining shapely streamline contour with large capacity. All-metal permanent Triumph badge. Flush rubber-mounted illuminated instrument panel carrying oil gauge, ammeter, switch and dash lamp. Quick opening filler cap. Capacity 3¼gal.

Oil Tank   All-steel welded with accessible filters, drain plug and separate vent: capacity ¾gal.

Frame   Brazed full cradle type, from tubes of finest alloy steel combining immense strength with lightness and correct weight distribution. Large diameter tapered front down tube. A comfortable riding position with the highest possible standard of roadholding at speed is secured.

Front Forks   Taper tube girder incorporating dampers with finger adjustment on the lower bridge.

Gearbox   Four-speed all-Triumph design and manufacture. Gears and shafts of nickel chrome steel of Triumph accuracy and precision. Large multi-plate clutch, patented positive-stop foot change.

Transmission   Primary chain running in polished cast aluminium oil bath of streamline design. Rear chain adequately protected.

Brakes   Triumph 7in diameter brakes with special alloy detachable ribbed drums and extra wide shoes. Finger adjustment. Front brake adjustment accessible from saddle.

Saddle   De luxe soft top type, adjustable for height.

Handlebar   Triumph, resiliently mounted, eliminating fatigue and shocks, full range of adjustment provided. Control levers grouped and adjustable to suit individual requirements. TT type brake and clutch levers.

Mudguards   Of adequate width with streamline section stays. Detachable tail-piece to facilitate wheel removal.

Wheels & Tyres   Latest Triumph wheels with spokes of approximately equal length taking braking and transmission stresses. Dunlop Universal tyres, front 26 x 3in ribbed, rear 26 x 3.50in studded.

Toolbox   Large capacity and watertight. All steel construction, rubber-sealed. Complete set of good quality tools, grease gun and instruction booklets.

Finish & Equipment   Entirely finished in Amaranth (dark) Red. Petrol tank finished in chromium plate with Amaranth panels lined out in gold. Spokes and rims chromium-plated, rim centres Amaranth lined out in gold. Specially shaped kneegrips for comfort and security at high speeds. Lucas 6 volt Magdyno lighting with voltage control, 8in diameter chromium plated anti glare headlamp, Altette horn. Chromium-plated downswept exhaust pipes. All aluminium parts smooth and highly polished and both chromium plate and enamel of highest quality. All nuts Cadmium plated.

joining the company I swapped the girder fork six-stud for a new telescopic eight-stud which was a big improvement, especially in the areas of comfort and handling. The early twin did get a little 'hairy' at high speed, particularly if the road surface was indifferent. Edward Turner would never admit this when you complained, which was natural I suppose. After all, he had designed it! Later on, when the 650 engine was being developed, the works put one in my bike to get some mileage on an experimental engine and

The Speed Twin engine. Simple, symmetrical and easy to manufacture. In service it was very reliable and maintenance presented no problems – it was as simple as a single.

that transformed the performance. The effect of that extra 150cc was quite remarkable.

Eric Headlam

Eric Headlam was a salesman of considerable presence and charm whose territory was London and the south of England. In addition to his normal sales duties, Eric, being in London, usually masterminded events like the Export Banquets at the Dorchester Hotel which we had from time to time. Stunts like the 'Gaffers Gallop' also came under his wing when he would reconnoitre routes and fix up hotel accommodation as well as escorting the riders.

Headlam's most important single customer was London's Metropolitan Police Force who, in 1938, invited all the leading motorcycle manufacturers to submit models for test, as they proposed to renew their fleet. The story goes that, on the day, the tests had just about finished but no Triumphs had arrived. They did so, literally at the last moment, with Turner and Headlam in attendance. The bike submitted was, of course, the new Speed Twin. Despite the lateness, the police agreed to put the twin through the test routine and it came top of the class much to the chagrin, no doubt, of its competitors.

Subsequently, Eric Headlam spent a lot of time each year at Scotland Yard and at the Police College in Hendon liaising with the various officers concerned with the Triumph motorcycle fleet, which eventually numbered several hundred.

'Studs'

The reference to 'six-stud' and 'eight-stud', for those not in the know, is the number of studs with nuts holding down the base of the cylinder block on the Triumph twin engine. As originally produced, it had just six studs and it was found that when pressed to the limit for a lengthy period, the block tended to lift off. The extra two studs introduced the following year cured this little embarrassment. It was not really a serious problem and used normally, no trouble would be experienced, as is proved by the not inconsiderable number of pre-war 'six-stud' models still running around. (What a price they fetch too!)

An interesting shot taken in the Priory Street works in 1939 when the new Speed Twin was on the assembly track. The machine (which can just be seen on the left behind the three hanging exhaust pipes) is a Speed Twin prototype which is still on the road today.

The advent of the Speed Twin was a landmark in motorcycle design. Not only was it the forerunner of a long line of Triumph twin engines of various sizes – 250, 350, 500, 650 and 750cc – which powered the range for the next thirty years, but it also set off a revolution in all the other factories, both in the UK and abroad. They all had to produce something similar in order to compete. This they did, but not until after the war and it is interesting to note the different ways they got round the various Triumph patents relating to the design.

BSA and Norton reverted to the old Val Page 6/1 layout with a single camshaft at the rear of the block and unequal-length pushrods. Matchless introduced a centre bearing for the crankshaft. (This was an expensive luxury not considered necessary by Triumph and from all accounts

Bert Hopwood, who, from Chief Engineer became Deputy Managing Director.

Bert Hopwood

Bert Hopwood was an old associate of Edward Turner from Ariel days, where they worked together for many years. Val Page moved from Ariel to Triumph in 1932 and Hopwood took over as Chief Draughtsman. Then in 1936, when Turner went to Triumph, Hopwood went with him as Design Assistant. He worked with Turner on the new twins which set the company on the road to success. He moved to Norton in 1947, BSA two years later, back to Norton in 1956 and finally to Triumph again in 1961. In the late sixties he was responsible, along with Development Engineer Doug Hele, for the introduction of the celebrated three-cylinder Triumph Trident (and its BSA counterpart the Rocket 3) which in race trim dominated the production racing scene almost to the exclusion of all rivals for several years. He was much involved in the problems that beset the industry in the seventies when he was Deputy Managing Director of the BSA Automotive Division. These traumatic days are fully described in a book he wrote after retirement, entitled *Whatever Happened to the British Motorcycle Industry?*

did not result in the vibration-free running that was expected.) Royal Enfield and Ariel offered different configurations and the Japanese, on some models at least, employed a 180deg crank as opposed to having the pistons moving in unison.

Yes, it was certainly a landmark and a very good one for the industry as a whole. 'The bark of a well tuned single' may have been music to the ear of the keen motorcyclist, but it was anathema to the general public. The twins that took to the roads after the war were generally well silenced and did not cause the kind of disturbance in peaceful surburban areas that was common at one time when big singles were the vogue. The image of motorcycling benefited greatly thereby.

Bert Coles, John McDonnell and Syd Tubb

On the production side we had Bert Coles (Works Manager John McDonnell (Production Manager) and Syd Tubb (Assembly). These three were a powerful trio who went about their business of ensuring that the right number of bikes came off the track each week. Bert had a good rapport with the unions and any problems were usually settled in his office once the Woodbines had been handed round! McDonnell (Mac to everyone) kept the components flowing to the tracks and in his spare time was a Coventry City Councillor. This enabled us, through him, to call on the Lord Mayor to greet any distinguished visitors we might have at the works (e.g. Johnny Allen) ensuring good publicity locally. Syd Tubb was in charge of assembly; the tracks were his babies and the testers reported to him.

That Triumph maintained such a high standard of quality over the years was very much due to these three and their staffs, who were the last to handle the product before the customer took delivery. Syd Tubb, by the way, rode in the 1913 Junior TT in the Isle of Man on a Humber, but regrettably retired, reason unknown.

Bert Coles.

John McDonnell, known as 'Mac'.

Syd Tubb.

Freddie Clarke

F W S Clarke was in charge of the Experimental Department. He was a well known and very successful performer at Brooklands – that great concrete bowl near Weybridge, now alas, no more. However, there is still some activity on the site, or what is left of it, reunions of men and machines and, I believe, sprints up the Test Hill which still remains. I rode there myself pre-war at a couple of Clubman meetings organized by *The Motor Cycle* magazine. My mounts were KSS Velocettes of which I was very fond.

Freddie Clarke joined Triumph in 1937 to head up an engine development section. Two years later, on a dope-burning Tiger 80, he set a new 350cc lap record at Brooklands at 105.97mph (170.53kph). Not content with this, and using a Tiger 100 bored out to 503cc, he lapped at 118.02mph (189.92kph) which took the 750cc class record. The 500cc record was already held by Ivan Wicksteed on a blown twin at exactly the same speed. With Brooklands closed for ever, these Triumph records will stand for all time.

Clarke, naturally, became heavily involved in the early development of the Triumph twin engines and Edward Turner had a very high opinion of his abilities. Freddie was a powerful character who stated his own views very clearly and on such days, no one, not even Turner, could move him! However, get him out of the works and put a pint in his hand and he was a different man!

The Riley Connection?

It has been said that the inspiration for the concept of Turner's parallel twin-cylinder engine came from the Riley 9 car engine. Turner owned one of these in the thirties and was very impressed with its design and performance. There is in fact quite a resemblance between the Riley and the Triumph in that both had separate camshafts (inlet and exhaust) mounted on opposite sides of the cylinder block. They were mounted high up so that the valves could be operated by quite short pushrods, so reducing the load on the valve gear.

How true this Riley theory is, no one can tell now and it is not really of any consequence – most designs are developments or modifications of something that has gone beforehand. Both the Triumph and the Riley were very good engines and the Triumph was in production from 1937 (excluding World War II) until the last 750s out of Meriden during the reign of the Co-op in the early eighties. It must have been the longest continuous production run of any engine in the British motorcycle industry.

Tiger 100

In 1939 a new sporting version of the Speed Twin was announced – the Tiger 100. It was the ultimate addition to the existing Tiger range and replaced the Tiger 90. This was the commencement of a policy adopted by Turner which he followed throughout the rest of his time with Triumph. It was to produce first a touring model, then follow it a year or so later with a hotted-up version. The Tiger 100 was identical to the Speed Twin as far as the general specification was concerned, but the compression ratio was stepped up to 8:1, with forged slipper type pistons.

Other features included polished internals and enhanced gas flow throughout. An aluminium-bronze cylinder head could be had for an extra £5. The finish was the same as the single-cylinder Tigers – silver sheen with blue lining and lots of chromium plate. It was offered at £80 (£5 more than the Speed Twin).

The Last Link

The year 1938 saw the disposal of the original Much Park Street premises in Coventry which Bettmann and Schulte

Tiger 100, 1939 – the hotted-up version of the Speed Twin. After the war, kits of racing parts were available which made the Tiger a really competitive competitor.

had bought in 1889 for their first manufacturing operation. The Service Department which had been located there was moved into the main factory.

7

War and Triumph

The year 1939 saw the outbreak of war once more, and as in 1914, the Government wanted motorcycles for the armed forces – urgently. They requisitioned machines from wherever they could find them – manufacturers and dealers' shops were stripped of their stocks, everything was taken, irrespective of whether the machines were suitable or not.

I was a Territorial at the time, and I was in at the start as a despatch rider. Our section sergeant, who did not know a Manx Norton from a BSA Bantam, did the requisitioning for us. He just went off with a 3-ton truck to dealers in the nearest town, probably Watford, and came back with it full of all different makes: Norton, Velocette, Ariel, BSA, Rudge, Triumph and AJS amongst others. We grabbed our favourite make (someone got the Triumph before I could, so I ended up with a very nice MAC Velo). We used these for a few weeks until being issued with new WD 16H Nortons. These again only lasted a short while and were replaced with 250cc side-valve BSAs. You can imagine the reaction in a bunch of hard-riding motorcyclists, used to handling powerful 500s! Whose brainwave it

was in the War Office to buy 250 side-valves will never be known. The poor little things did not last long; they seized with monotonous regularity and gradually fell apart.

To get back to Triumph, all finished machines in stock in the factory were taken, and everything produced thereafter of 350cc and over, was requisitioned, including Speed Twins and Tiger 100s. In all, 1,400 machines were dispatched within six weeks of the outbreak of war. Full production of the 350cc side-valve as selected by the War Office continued until January 1940, when the programme was reduced on Government instructions. In the first half of 1940, reduced military requirements made it possible to produce several thousand machines for Home and Export markets. In March, contracts were finalized with the French Government for the supply of 500cc side-valves and deliveries were made in two to three weeks. Other production in this period included large quantities of aircraft components, tank track links, steering housings and two-wheeled stretcher carriages. Machine tool work was also undertaken for other manufacturers.

In 1938 a specification for a military motorcycle had

been issued and Triumph, Matchless, Royal Enfield and BSA were asked to submit prototypes. This called for an engine not less than 250cc and weight not to exceed 250lb (113kg). Turner started with the 350cc twin engine that would have been in the Model 3T for 1939, attached a three-speed gearbox, a light frame, girder forks, and for the first time on any kind of vehicle – an alternator to supply current for lighting. After the war, larger alternators replaced magnetos and dynamos on motorcycles and were adopted universally for cars as well.

The authorities, after testing, gave the green light to produce the 3TW (as it was designated) and the factory started work on a batch of fifty. There was even some talk about it becoming the standard services motorcycle and that all manufacturers would make it. This never happened for reasons which will be clear in a moment.

In May 1940 civilian and export production ceased and full production of military machines was resumed and by July, output was up to 300 machines a week. In October, air raids affected the output to some extent, including a complete close-down for several days, whilst a large, delayed action bomb was removed from the enamelling shop. Aircraft component output was maintained throughout this period. Development of the 350cc twin was completed during the year and a power-driven winch for installation in target towing aircraft was developed for the Ministry of Aircraft Production, using the 500cc twin engine. This engine was also used in a portable generator set for the Air Ministry to supply power on Lancaster and Halifax bombers for the radar.

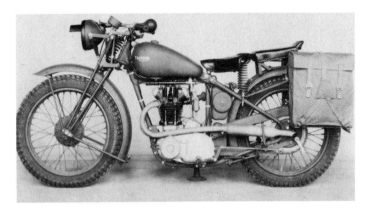

Turner's design for the Services, the ill-fated 3TW, which was destroyed in the Coventry blitz.

Disaster!

On 14 November 1940, a small number of the batch of fifty 3TWs had been completed and the remainder were on their way down the track. It was the night that the German air force was launched on a mission to obliterate Coventry – major producer of all kinds of military hardware, guns, tanks, vehicles, aircraft, aircraft engines and much more. A fair military target, one might say. The number of planes taking part was reckoned to be at least 400 and their target was the city centre.

They found it. In the morning, it was a smoking ruin and this included the Triumph Priory Street works which was located in the centre, just a stone's throw away from the cathedral. Triumph employees on night shift took to the shelters when the sirens went and remarkably no lives

were lost. In the city was a different story: 554 people had been killed, 865 seriously injured, including twenty-six firemen killed and 200 injured. Seventy-five per cent of the city's industry had been seriously damaged as had over 46,000 houses. After the raid there was neither water, gas nor electricity. It was the end of the 3TW.

I saw this dreadful event from a distance, as I was on my way (on the Speed Twin) to see my parents in North Wales and had put up in Evesham for the night. The flames over Coventry, nearly forty miles away, could be clearly seen.

So what was the Triumph position next day? No factory, no tools, no production.

Shambles at Priory Street. The morning after the November blitz on Coventry. Remains of some of the ill-fated new 3TW model for the Services can be seen in the wreckage.

Waiting to go off! A large, unexploded bomb which awaited the factory staff on the morning after – it was safely defused.

A grotesque statue of girders after the bombing.

Salvage operations commenced promptly. An old foundry in Warwick (seven miles away) was converted into a machine shop and production of Army service parts was started. It was uphill work with very limited accommodation, but progress was made and by June 1941, complete machines were coming off the track once more. Edward Turner moved to BSA around this time; no reason has ever been given for this move as far as I know.

However, the machines coming off the track were not

The 'Tin Tabernacle' in Warwick, where Triumph set up production after the blitz. The motorcycles are OHV and side-valve 350s.

The ultimate Triumph motorcycle for the Services – the 3HW, an OHV 350 developed from pre-war 3H.

only the side-valvers that had been produced previously, but OHV 350s based on the pre-war 3H, and renamed 3HW. The only major difference was that whereas the 3H and Tiger 80 had separate alloy rocker boxes, the 3HW rocker boxes were cast integrally with the head. I had one of these in Burma and a very nice little model it was too, very similar to my pre-war Tiger 80. There was only one problem with it in Burma – the dust soon put paid to the bore and rings, no air cleaner being fitted. A couple of thousand miles was about the limit before major servicing was required. The same thing happened to the G3/L Matchlesses that we had.

Why no air cleaners were fitted to bikes going into appallingly dusty conditions is a question that could only be answered by some official in Whitehall, I suppose. Maybe he was not even aware that it was dusty in the dry season in that part of the world. I'll warrant the Japanese had air cleaners!

To Fresh Fields

Triumph could not continue to operate efficiently in a semi-derelict foundry in Warwick and management minds were much concentrated on the long-term future – when the war was over. Popular opinion was that the old factory should be rebuilt. Some of it was still there, things like services and even foundations. However, the War Damage Commission considered that Priory Street was too much in the target area for future attacks. Also, the city

fathers had plans for the development of the centre after the war which did not include big factories cluttering up the area around the cathedral.

The directors were therefore forced to look for a new site. Eventually, one was decided upon between Allesley and Meriden on the main Coventry–Birmingham road (A45). This was what is referred to in today's planning terms as a 'green field site', meaning that it had been inhabited only by sheep and cattle up to that time. This decision raised a bit of a furore in Meriden village, not without some justification.

However, there was a war on and Whitehall gave the go-ahead. Work on the site commenced in July and by March 1942 some machinery was actually installed and in operation. Within a short time, the factory became a self-contained unit once more and quantity output an actual fact. The transfer to Meriden was completed without any noticeable effect on output which was governed at this time by available labour, but was nevertheless raised to nearly 11,000 machines in 1944. Huge quantities of spares were also produced representing between twenty-five and thirty per cent of the factory capacity.

The total number of motorcycles produced for the forces was 49,700, which is a remarkable figure when you take into account the interruption caused by the destruction of the factory. There was also a wide range of other military products which have already been mentioned.

For World War I, 30,000 motorcycles were produced at Priory Street.

8

Triumph and America

In the post-war period, the biggest market for Triumph was the United States of America. It is interesting and instructive to see how this came about, since before the war there was virtually no motorcycle market in the States – the two indigenous manufacturers (Indian and Harley Davidson) making very big, heavy twin-cylinder machines used mainly by the police. Indian eventually faded out after attempting to make a vertical twin on Triumph lines and only Harley was left.

The death of Bill Johnson Jnr, President and founder of Johnson Motors Inc of Pasadena California, on 4 March 1962, marked the end of a chapter in the remarkable story of the British motorcycle in America – a story in the best traditions of British commerce overseas. This chapter in the history of Triumph covers a period of about twenty-five years, in which the US was converted from a non-existent market to the biggest importer of British machines in the world.

Bill Johnson was the true pioneer behind this remark-able achievement and his own success story reads like a romance. A lawyer by profession, he married in 1934 when just out of Law School and whilst on honeymoon in Hawaii came across an Ariel dealer who happened to have one of the famous Square Fours in stock. A keen motor-cyclist, and with more than a smattering of engineering knowledge, Johnson was attracted to this machine, bought it and took it back home to California.

Then followed some correspondence with the Ariel factory in England and the designer of the machine, Edward Turner. Johnson suggested that he might be able to sell Ariels on the West Coast and with nothing to lose, the Ariel factory appointed him as a distributor.

In 1936, Edward Turner joined Triumph as Managing Director and designed the famous Speed Twin and Tiger 100 vertical twins. Bill Johnson was persuaded to add the Triumph range to his franchise and at the outbreak of war was selling a small but steady quantity of both Ariel and Triumph models.

It must be appreciated that at this time motorcycling was virtually a defunct sport in America, so that Johnson had to sell the sport to his customers as well as the machines. Contact was maintained during the war years and in 1945 Edward Turner made the first of his many annual visits to the US and met Bill Johnson personally. A close friendship developed and from that time, the Triumph business in America rose in a spectacular manner and in doing so encouraged other manufacturers, both British and foreign, to come in.

The American motorcycle movement became really big business – not in the American sense, but certainly as far as European manufacturers were concerned. In 1960 alone, Bill Johnson's organization imported over 3,000 Triumph motorcycles and over the years the value of his imports has totalled many millions of dollars.

'Contact was Maintained During the War'

I wrote this in the previous paragraph and I can now amplify it with extracts from letters written by Edward Turner to Bill Johnson during those years.

4 March 1941

I am glad to say that considerable progress has been made, particularly in regard to the production of spare

Bill Johnson, boss of Johnson Motors Inc of California, who played a major part in establishing a market in the US which eventually absorbed most of Meriden's output. The 'Cigar' is Johnny Allen's first record-breaker which clocked 193mph (310kph) on the Salt Flats in the background.

parts, and by the time you read this letter we shall be in a position to execute all orders outstanding for spare parts.

With reference to the Indian agency situation, I am naturally very pleased that you are not likely to be intimidated by Hitler methods of this sort, and I can only give you my assurance that your pioneer efforts on our behalf will be amply repaid after the war, if not before, by the continuance of our support in the form of bigger and better supplies of good selling machines.

As regards Sammett & Blair, it is news to me that they have issued a bulletin to the effect that our factory has been bombed. This is very indiscreet of them, particularly as we have been asked to avoid news of this kind in our foreign correspondence, and the only point in our doing so is in our dealers' interests, to let them know how they stand.

10 May 1941

At the moment of writing, things seem to be moving in regard to more active participation in this war of the US and frankly I should be very thrilled if they would come in altogether in a naval sense, as it would enable the US to have a say in the peace settlement, and at the same time bring the British Empire and the US closer together, which would undoubtedly benefit the whole world.

I am glad to say that the batteries and tubes you dispatched to me all arrived safely, for which many thanks. It also indicates that the Battle of the Atlantic is not going too unfavourably.

As I think I mentioned in my previous letters, the next time I visit the US which I hope will be soon after this war, I intend to journey to California and look you up, although I fear it will be some considerable time yet, but nevertheless it is a pleasant thought for the future.

3 June 1941

Referring to your cable of 17 May, re gears, which read as follows:

DEFENCE PROGRAM MAKES IT IMPOSSIBLE TO HAVE GEARS MADE HERE STOP TRIUMPHS RENDERED USELESS UNTIL GEARS REPLACED STOP NEED MOST URGENTLY MAINSHAFT HIGH GEARS AND LAYSHAFT HIGH GEARS STOP CAN USE ONE HUNDRED EACH BY POST STOP PLEASE ADVISE.

to which we have replied as follows:

REFERENCE YOUR CABLE 17th ONLY JUST RESUMED MANUFACTURE IN SMALL WAY BUT WE WILL DO OUR BEST TO LET YOU HAVE SOME GEARS WITHIN FOURTEEN DAYS.

I am pleased to be able to say that we shall be able to let you have a quantity of fifty gears within fourteen days from now, although I fear it will take a month or so for them to reach you. This may not sound as favourable on time as you would wish, but bearing in mind the fact that our complete manufacturing plant was eliminated, and before we could resume manufacture we had practically to rebuild a derelict factory in a strange town, procure fresh plant, small tools and labour, I cannot feel that it is a bad show.

As a matter of interest, at the time of writing, we are just producing the first small quantity of machines for the British Government, after one of the worst write-offs in industrial history.

7 July 1941

I am pleased to say that we have already dispatched a small number of gears, to be followed by a larger quantity soon after. I am rather puzzled as to why you should need these gears, as from our records you have handled just over 300 of our machines, and the spares you are ordering seem to be extremely high in proportion to the machines in service. We ourselves have experienced so little trouble with our gearbox from the wear point of view, that we can only assume that these replacements are required because of gear failures.

If this is so, you can almost certainly look to the bushes moving axially out of position, which would, of course, remove the support from the pair of gears taking the stress and cause the shafts to bend, which in turn would allow the gears to operate out of their proper mesh, which would inevitably lead to failure. I know we struck a patch of trouble some years ago, with faulty porous bronze bushes, but I am only passing on this information, as to remove the cause of the trouble is much better than removing the result.

I am glad you have found something interesting in my article in the *British Export Journal* which, by the way, was sent to you more to introduce you to the journal itself, which might be of some interest, as I am aware that the article was not written strictly in accordance with what I know to be the requirements of the US markets. If only it were possible to design a machine for each particular market, we should indeed do some export business, but for a company even of the size that ours was it is rarely possible to have more than two machines of fundamental dissimilarity in one's range, although we managed to produce ten models out of two machines and several engines.

I certainly have given a very considerable amount of thought to post-war export problems, and I hope to be in the running with a suitable line, immediately the war ends; but the future of the world, its economic structure, its fiscal barriers and its exporting facilities are so uncertain at the moment that the prizes will go to those who are smart enough to get a move on as soon as the situation begins to clarify, as the best laid schemes of the moment are likely to go astray.

In regard to the short list of the most urgent spares required, contained in your letter of 26 June I have passed this to our Service Manager and asked him to personally progress these. I am sure I have your indulgence, as you know our circumstances.

15 August 1941

Please reply to: The Cape, Warwick

Further to your letter of 26 June I have now had an opportunity of studying the excellent print you have sent me of the scooter that you have designed, and also the Salzbury *Motor Glide* catalogue, which you kindly enclosed.

With regard to the excellent job which you have made in

your own workshops, I can only say that it appears to be very workmanlike, and the fact that it will do over 50mph [80kph] is proof of its all-round efficiency. The whole point about this sort of proposition, however, rests with whether this type of vehicle has any real future. I believe it has, if it is sufficiently light in construction to be parked in the household, or at any rate if it does not require a garage.

The other requirements of such a vehicle are – to be infallibly reliable in the hands of a non-technical owner; to start really easily, and to be simple to control; but I cannot help feeling that by the time one has achieved all this, one has arrived at a vehicle which costs almost as much as a motorcycle.

This may not be a disadvantage that would rule it out from a commercial point of view, since it gives an illusion, at any rate, of being much safer to ride than a motorcycle.

I notice in this week's edition of *The Motor Cycle* that some space is devoted to describing your vehicle, with a photograph of yourself seated on it, which makes very interesting reading. If it is your intention to manufacture these in any quantity, I should be glad to know how this is received in America.

I notice that the Salzbury *Motor Glide* has rather cunning gear transmission in the form of a primary 'V' rubber belt, and I have always thought that this very simple means of changing the gear ratios has advantages, provided that it is only asked to transmit low power. As a matter of fact, in giving a certain amount of thought to post-war development of an ultra-lightweight and cheap motorcycle, we had thought of a similar kind of transmission.

At the moment of writing we have just heard of Mr Roosevelt meeting with Winston Churchill at sea and, although the declaration of joint war-aims as a result of this meeting is not exactly news to us, I have no doubt that they took the opportunity of discussing more far-reaching decisions of action to be taken by the two countries in the event of the Japs getting out of hand.

My own opinion is now that the surprising resistance the Russians have put up to the German invasion has turned the scales of the war, and although it may well be that they will over-run a large slice of Russia, they will have lost so much of their resources in doing so that it may well make all the difference between victory and defeat in the ultimate issue.

We are turning out a few more machines for the Government, although our total production is still in our temporary works – a pale shadow of our former large scale production – and I am sorry to say that it will be some years before this company really recovers from the losses it has sustained, but the progress to date is very good indeed and when we remove to our new factory, with augmented plant, we shall once more be able to get down to our previous flourishing business.

Note: The Cape Warwick was where production resumed after the blitz. It was a derelict foundry and corrugated iron chapel, known as 'The Tin Tabernacle'.

3 September 1941

With regard to your letter of 17th enclosing particulars of the Powell 'Aviate' scooter and the 'Servi-Cycle', I have examined both of these with interest. As you say, the Powell looks a bit of a mess! The thing that intrigues me about it however, is the blatant compromise of the whole thing, for sale in a country which has been trained over a number of years to expect the best from all mechanical products. I should be extremely surprised if these continued to sell, although I suppose one would need to see and ride it to arrive at a definite conclusion.

With regard to the 'Servi-Cycle', this is much more stereotyped, and it is interesting to see that it uses a 2-belt drive, a system which would not be tolerated in this country on the most simple motorcycle.

It would appear that generally interest is reviving in the States in the motorcycle. Although I have not been in very close touch, I have not seen so much evidence for many years of motorcycle activity. I hope it continues, as I have always felt that the reason for the decline of motorcycle popularity in the States, is the fact that the industry has resolved into two firms, who have been pre-occupied in fighting each other instead of attracting custom and broadening the scope of motorcycles. If you had a dozen makes doing reasonable business, I am sure it would stimulate an interest in motorcycling as a pastime. I well remember the interest with which I used to study the Reading–Standard, Henderson, Cleveland, and other makes in times gone by, and they always appealed to me, for their rugged strength and their general lines seemed to personify enormous power.

There is great work to be done in America in bringing the youth back to motorcycles, as in my opinion this is a very manly sport for which there is no real substitute. Certainly they do not get much of a kick out of a 'flivver'. I only wish we were in a position to supply you with several hundreds of our twins a year, as I am sure it would more nearly hit the target than any other machine at the present time, particularly if we could ship them over at a considerably lower price than has been possible heretofore. I do not know, of course, where the economics of the democracies are drifting, and it is to be hoped that the pound and the dollar will remain in something like the same relationship as it was pre-war.

9 October 1941

You may be interested to know that our new factory is well on the way to completion and we hope to be manufacturing motorcycles once again in large quantities early in the New Year. Although these will all be devoted to the war effort, we are by no means losing sight of the requirements of our export market immediately this is again possible.

There is every indication that next year will be the crucial year in this gigantic struggle, and I think the back of the job will be broken towards the end of that year. In the meantime, I hope that your business is still reasonably good in the difficult circumstances . . .

Mystery 350 Twins

The letter quoted below was written by Edward Turner, but is not addressed to America this time. However, it is very interesting as it refers to two 350 twins for the military and is dated October 1941. This was almost twelve months after the blitz which destroyed the first (and only) batch of 3TW twins. Maybe these two machines had been built somehow from blitzed parts with a view to setting the project on its way again. They might also have been prototypes of the 3T de Luxe due to be launched in September 1939 and postponed due to the war? The letter is included here to keep it in chronological date order with the American letters.

Lieutenant-Colonel C Barker
Headquarters
11th Armoured Division
Home Forces

29 October 1941

Dear Colonel Barker,

I must thank you for your letter of 25th inst re the 350 twin. I note that it will not be possible for your General to inspect this until after 20 November, and this is satisfactory, as the only two twins in existence at the moment are both dismantled for a modification in the form of a larger mag-generator which will give a brighter light, and furthermore they have since been equipped with the pannier bag-cum-pillion equipment with which you are no doubt familiar.

When these modifications are complete they are going to be retested at MEE so that it will probably be more convenient to send one up for your inspection before these tests start. I therefore will hold one in readiness for a two- or three-day visit to your Headquarters, and I shall expect to hear from you on or after 20 November.

I am at present out of action having, of all things, been afflicted with the palsy, but I am hoping that I shall be fit well before 20 November, in which case I should be very pleased to come up as your guest for the night, if only to renew our acquaintance.

Kindest regards

[I find the reference to a 'brighter light' rather strange as headlamps were masked during the war and the amount of light permitted was microscopic, why would ET want anything brighter?]

Now, back to the letters to Bill Johnson Jnr.

9 December 1941

I am answering your last letter of 4 November at a time which is fateful in American history, as we have just heard of Japan's declaration of war, preceded by their treacherous attack on your various bases in the Pacific.

Of course, this had to come, and it is probably better for the US and Britain that it should come now than at any other time. Our only hope over here is, naturally, that it will not diminish the aid to Britain which we so sorely need. I must say that it seems a suicidal act on the part of Japan, and there is no doubt that there will be considerable fighting before it is all over and considerable losses to the US, since what the Japs may lack in technique in modern warfare they undoubtedly make up with fanaticism, which has always been a tremendous asset throughout the conflicts of mankind. Bravery and valour is one thing, but that blind fanaticism of the semi-civilized which enables a man to meet death with a smile, secure, as he thinks, in the knowledge that he is going to a form of paradise that only heroes can enter, is another. To some extent, this primitive instinct is still a characteristic of the Germans which has enabled them to make such a good showing in this war up to now, with such appalling losses.

The end of all this is inevitable. It must mean the ultimate collapse of the Axis. Although America is not officially at war with Germany yet, I hope that this will follow before long, as it will clean up the books and reduce the whole situation to a clean issue between the US, USSR and British Empire against the Axis and their dupes.

These are tremendously interesting times, although so tragic, and on the whole, I cannot help feeling it is a good thing for America that the Pacific menace is at last brought to an issue. A nation finds its soul in war, and I have not the slightest doubt that the US will, in years to come, benefit by their being tried in the flame of this war. Production, however, it is quite obvious, is the key to the whole situation, even more than man-power and certainly more than wealth, since we have now at long last learnt that wealth is the productive power of men rather than gold. The production of this country is magnificent; much more than one would think by listening to all the grumbles and so on, and by the middle of next year it will undoubtedly reach tremendous proportions. I can only hope that the US will make short work of the Japs . . . as it will undoubtedly clear the way for the final assault on Germany.

Having got that off my chest it seems rather small talk to revert to motorcycles, but nevertheless these are our main business when all's said and done, and I am afraid that my news in this direction is rather doleful, as we are finding increasing difficulty in obtaining Export Permits for spare parts and you can imagine how I feel at not being able to supply you with the spares that I know you need.

The name DuPont has always been associated with General Motors in this country, and I assume that this is the same family, as I understood they own a controlling interest in the Indian factory. It looks as though your friend Stephen DuPont has been collecting quite an array of English motorcycles – not to mention the German BMW – with a view to producing something similar in the Indian concern, and I have no doubt that that small percentage of US trade that has fallen to British manufacturers will be even more difficult to maintain after the war.

Do you think that high speed racing has much effect on general motorcycle sales in America? Or . . . is it necessary to support racing from a Triumph standpoint, since we are only selling to the individualist sportsman? Because we have rather set our face against a racing policy, being content to produce an exceptionally fast machine for sale rather than for the purpose of winning a few races to help our standard stuff along.

12 January 1942

I began receiving a weekly copy of *Life* long before your card arrived announcing that you have been kind enough to make a present to me of the subscription . . .

The comprehensive impression of American life that this book conveys, makes one's mouth water at the moment, but at least it serves as a reminder of the good times which may lie ahead of us when the present international brigands have been got under control.

Again thanking you, and wishing you an easy passage through the difficulties that lie ahead.

19 January 1942

With regard to spares, you can rely on our giving you the best service we can, and I understand eighty-six sets of gears have already been dispatched to you. We are about to dispatch another batch before long which we have managed to put through with an Army order by increasing the quantities slightly. I understand also that we are awaiting an Export Licence for gearbox cases, so the situation does not look too bad. I am very pleased to hear that not a single parcel was lost in transit, as this is significant.

With regard to the war – as things have turned out, the Japanese aggression may be a blessing in disguise, as it not only serves to unite your country over the issue, but will make the majority of small Americans who have no appreciation of America's obligations outside her own territory, realize that any nation that is great must from time to time stand up and fight, not only for its own rights, but for the rights of the system to which it subscribes.

I must say, I was a little bit nervous of the possibility of American public opinion being guided along the lines of thinking that they were pulling the British chestnuts out of the fire, and now we are Allies in the true sense of the word, with our own particular problems and objectives. It will no doubt make a great difference to American life, as it has to ours, but after a year or more of this unpleasantness, we should be able to get back to legitimate business and building up a better world for everyone to live in . . .

In conclusion, please rest assured that I will do everything possible in our present difficult circumstances to give you an adequate supply of spares. It would help us quite a lot if you could get out some sort of forecast of your requirements for the next twelve months, so that we could give the Works plenty of notice to enable them to slip us non-standard spares. (We are no longer making Twins.)

[There is a gap here of over eighteen months when Edward Turner left Triumph and joined BSA. The correspondence with Bill Johnson resumed on Turner's return to Triumph.]

1 September 1943

I have rejoined Triumph Engineering in my old capacity: I have no doubt that this will be of interest to you, and probably the news will not be unwelcome inasmuch that I know you put in a considerable amount of work in marketing both Triumph and Ariel machines. I shall also be interested in Ariel, inasmuch that their post-war design policy will be in my hands . . .

I am writing to Mr Salzbury separately and I am glad to say that this new change in my business life will not necessarily prevent me from proceeding with the project discussed regarding an industrial air-cooled engine, although for the time being I shall not be able to do much about this. I propose however, to let Mr Salzbury have my views in regard to the most desirable type of engine for his

The Triumph factory at Meriden (Warwickshire) just after building had been completed in 1942. Not much activity to be seen.

purpose together with a general arrangement after I have settled down and got on top of the situation at Triumph.

You may or may not be aware that Triumph Engineering is now fully installed in its new factory, and though not quite such a husky baby as it was, it has every facility for becoming bigger and better than ever. The new factory, which was necessary owing to the complete destruction of the old, has been designed and laid out on most modern lines for the specific purpose of economic manufacture of quality motorcycles.

Although we are still fully engaged on machines for the Armed Forces, you may depend that the approach of peace will not find us napping, and you may look forward with confidence to having a very fine range of machines to handle in the US.

I will write to you further when I have had the opportunity of assimilating the correspondence between this company and your goodself over the last eighteen months since I have been away.

30 September 1943

A few days ago I was visited by Mr Christie of Messrs Scholefield, Goodman & Sons Ltd, Merchants & Shippers, Birmingham who informed me that they have had correspondence with you over the matter of handling your buying in this country.

I have known Messrs Scholefield Goodman & Sons Ltd for many years and Mr Christie is a thoroughly sound man.

It may be that their handling of the business between us will have certain advantages; at the same time, I should like to make it clear that we do not regard ourselves involved in this in any way. I imagine they approached you in the first place, and if this is the case, they have had no encouragement from Triumph.

Referring to the future, they pressed us to accept a token order on your behalf for 100 machines, which we have done, but I explained to them that it does not really mean anything since we are a long way off peace-time production. I would like to have your remarks on the foregoing, as I am anxious as to how the link-up of Messrs Scholefield Goodman & Sons Ltd and yourselves came about.

Regarding the future, I think I can safely promise that we can offer you very much increased territory in the US and although I would ask you not to take this as a commitment, if you can put up a suitable scheme which would satisfy us that you were able to satisfactorily exploit the whole of the US we would be prepared to consider this.

I personally feel that there are very good prospects of selling a large number of Triumph machines in the US after the war, because in spite of a natural desire on the part of your country to find work for their own industry, what would be to our mutual selves a large turnover would be relatively small taking the automotive industry as a whole, and I feel that our two Companies could do very big business before it would be regarded as in any way a menace. I leave in your very capable hands the correct approach to the American market with British machines, as I am sure you have a sound appreciation of the psychological and other factors of the market.

Referring to our post-war products, you will no doubt not be surprised when we tell you that the possibility of anything very new is not great to begin with, but you may depend on the Triumph programme being sound and attractive.

The advent of my return to the management of this company will not necessarily prevent my visit to the States, although it may delay it a little, as obviously I want to get things working smoothly in a difficult period before I leave it for a time.

I had words with Mr Goodwin of Ariel, over the telephone the other day, and I am glad to note that he speaks very favourably of your activities and in the event of our fixing up a comprehensive arrangement with you to handle our two makes, it is to be hoped that you will find it sufficiently adequate not to concern yourselves with other machines. However, this is all very much in the future, because although the news is very good indeed and the whole war situation in Europe is most favourable, I for one, do not feel we are on the eve of peace, although one always reserves the fact that anything can happen at any moment. At any rate, there will be certainly enough time to make all preparations for our 'peace offensive'.

I shall look forward with interest to a reply to this letter. Trusting you are keeping well, and that your present business is not involving you in too many complicated commitments.

2 December 1943

Referring to my letter of 30 September, in which I mentioned that I had received a visit from Mr Christie of Scholefield Goodman & Sons Ltd I might mention that I have not had any reply or any indication that you have received this, although you have since written to the company, dated 3 November. Would you kindly let me know whether you have received this letter, copy of which I enclose.

In regard to your letter of 3 November, we think it highly desirable in the interests of post-war trade to keep *Motorcyclist* alive, and we should imagine with the withdrawal of the support of Indian and Harley, the position is difficult with this journal. If you think it would serve any useful purpose to take a full page every month, or once in two months, for Triumph, we should be glad if you will do this and we shall, of course, credit your account at this end. I am asking Mr Welton to forward you copy and photographs from which blocks can be made.

I leave to your judgement the possibility of persistent advertising by British machines such as Triumph and Ariel in this journal being construed by our American competitors as an indication of a bold bid for motor cycle business in the US after the war, and although this is our intention with your goodselves, it is not always policy to advertise it beforehand. Therefore the desire to support the *Motorcyclist* must be weighed against the possibility of our stimulating an aggressive attitude on the part of American manufacturers. Perhaps you will let me have your views on this.

6 January 1944

Another shot of the shattered factory. It was astonishing how much machinery was retrieved from this disaster and restored to work again at Meriden.

With regard to South America, we had a tentative bid for this market, but with the high price of our machines contrasted by the exceedingly low prices of the German machines before this war, we did not get very far, although, of course, there were quite a number of enthusiasts who bought a few Triumphs but the whole business did not amount to much. We hope to be in a position to offer something more appropriate to this market after the war.

Awaiting your reply with interest.

I was very pleased to have your letter of 16 November, enclosing a copy of your previous letter of 29 July, because it so clearly explains how Messrs Scholefield Goodman & Sons Ltd came into the picture. You can imagine it was a surprise when this firm called on me soon after I returned to Triumph and began discussing your goodselves, which I do not wish you to take as in any way disapproving, since, as I said, it may have certain advantages, but in order to be able to assess this new situation I wonder if you would mind calculating just what Buying Commission would add to your retail price in America on the basis of considerably increased business post-war.

Our attitude with regard to shippers is naturally determined by whether their services justify their Buying Commission. In our Australian business, they do, and it may well be that they will also be useful to us both in our future operations in the US. The only objection we can possibly have is that it may increase the price of our products to the customer in the export market to an extent which would jeopardize demand. Now you are in the best position to assess this and your comments on the point would be most welcome. In any case it is a matter which should be cleared up without delay, as we do not wish to introduce any complications when we get going post-war.

May I take this opportunity of sincerely thanking you for the very handsome leather wallet which came safely to hand and which gave me great pleasure. It is a unique souvenir from the US for whom we all have very warm feelings, these days particularly, and also a kindly thought on your part which is much appreciated.

I have recently written to Mr Salzbury further on the engine situation and I am awaiting his reply. In the meantime please accept my best wishes for a happy and prosperous New Year.

7 April 1944

In answer to your letter of 17 February, I have given careful consideration to the contents and on the whole I think it will be to our mutual advantage to utilize the services that Messrs Scholefield, Goodman & Sons Ltd offer, as their 2½ per cent commission will not unduly load the price of our machines to the American buyers, particularly as there is already a considerable loading, and it may be that the volume of business we can do post-war will bring about a situation whereby the services that Messrs Scholefield Goodman offer, both in regard to shipping and finance, will be appreciated by both of us.

The particulars of how you arrive at your retail price and the terms on which you are selling to Dealers were, of course, very interesting to us, and they are approximately those on which the majority of our Australian business is done. I say 'approximately' because in actual fact the Australian margin is rather less. In view, however, of the advertising, racing, and general publicity expenses that you have to bear in relation to the relatively restricted market, we feel that your margin is strictly reasonable.

Naturally, we would like to obtain the largest share of business in the US after the war, and price to the consumer must always have an influence on the business obtained.

Speaking generally, the market for British motorcycles of particular types, such as the Triumph twin and the Ariel four, should be very large indeed after the war. We have had a surprising number of enquiries from all parts of the US during these last six months, and also had a visit from one or two soldiers who are either directly or indirectly connected with the business in the US and who have come to talk about post-war business. The signs are very clear that the interest in the British type of motorcycling is on the increase and with proper fostering can be worked up to very considerable proportions. At least, that is my view, and I have no doubt that you hold similar views.

I do not know how much competition we are likely to have from your two manufacturers, but as a matter of interest, there have been a large number of Harley-Davidsons, new and second-hand, offered for disposal over here, as the users now prefer British machines. I was a great admirer of American-made motorcycles for many years, but I am bound to admit that they have gone to sleep in recent years. Just how much the manufacturers will exert themselves after the war remains to be seen, but I should imagine they are no fools and if machines like the Triumph Speed Twin get away with a considerable amount of business I can see their policy changing and producing something very similar. However, this be as it may, the barometer is 'Set Fair' for us.

9

East Coast – West Coast

The correspondence continues with a letter from ET to Mr Sangster.

18 April 1944

Dear Mr Sangster,

With reference to my visit to Westfield Road today, may I thank you for the excellent lunch and for the opportunity of covering one or two points which were on my mind.

I enclose herewith my views on the letter and proposals of Alfred R Child.

Yours faithfully

Note: 77 Westfield Road was Mr Sangster's residence in Edgbaston, Birmingham.

The US and Alfred R Child

Whatever else Mr Child may have, he certainly has that invaluable asset for a commercial man, of being able to write a clear and a reasoned letter. No one could read this letter without being impressed by his possibilities, and although I agree with Mr Goodwin that we would be unwise to drop Johnson Motors in favour of this man, I do not agree with Goodwin's reasoning. Furthermore, I do not place any reliance on the views of the somewhat naive Mr Hopping with whom I had no contact in the US apart from our original meeting when we appointed him. Hopping can be dismissed from this matter as being an earnest young man with no experience, who came under the spell of Mr Johnson's undeniable personal charm.

I do not take the view that simply because Johnson Motors have made a success of the importation of British machines into California they are necessarily suitable or desirable to be entrusted with the exploitation of our machines for the whole of the US territory. I feel with Mr Alfred R Child that the possibilities for the sale of British machines in the US are very strong indeed and if a reasonable basis is created in the first place, this can grow into a very large market for our machines for many years to come.

Subject to the usual considerations and safeguards I would have no hesitation in entrusting Child with our representation in the US, were it not for the fact that we already have such a good man as Johnson, who thoroughly understands the psychology of the US motor cycle market and has his ear very close to the ground. He is of proven business ability, but all of this applies to him only as an agent or a regional distributor.

I believe that if the whole of the territory of the US were given to Johnson Motors, he would undoubtedly sell as many machines as we were prepared to release for the first year or two, but I am thinking of the years that lie ahead, when the mild boom likely to be experienced on both sides of the Atlantic will start to subside and we are in need essentially of good export orders at regular intervals, which can only be obtained from a nationwide distributor-ship.

In order to ensure the popularity of Triumph and Ariel machines in the US we need them on display in show-rooms in many towns in many states, which either means that Johnson Motors must find the capital for setting up depots or use the facilities of existing agents who can be induced to take an interest in British machines. These conditions rather favour Child as the Factory Representa-tive, if he can be interested in the proposition of operating for us on a moderate commission on total turnover, leaving Johnson Motors to concentrate on California and the West Coast with possibly, as a concession to his loyalty to us over difficult periods, the inclusion of Arizona, Nevada, Oregon and Washington.

If, on the other hand, Mr Child wishes to be appointed as sole importer for the US, much as it is suggested by Mr Goodwin that Child should so be appointed, my inclination would be to retain Johnson, as he at least, has a proven record.

I suggest, in answering Mr Child, that his reactions are obtained on the proposal that he represents Triumph and Ariel as Factory Representative on, say, a 3¾ or even five per cent commission on total turnover, retaining Johnson as a distributor, covering the aforementioned territory; this, of course, without committing ourselves in any way. I would not, however, feel inclined to clinch the deal until we have seen the man and, preferably, have visited the US once more, when conversations with Johnson would also be possible to get a better idea of what his facilities are for the exploitation of the US on a basis of continuity in the future.

In conclusion, Child's letter is that of a keen business man who seems to understand the motor cycle market, particularly in the US and he is too valuable a connection to dismiss lightly. Something should be done with him. It is just possible, however, that a man of his apparent calibre may not be interested in being purely a Factory Represen-tative.

[Edward Turner was obviously impressed with Alf Child but the latter did not, in the end, become involved with Triumph or Ariel, but as I recall, became the American East Coast distributor for BSA. On his retirement, many years later, his sales, spares, service and school organization at Nutley, New Jersey, was bought up by BSA. The question of how Triumph would develop their sales organization to embrace the whole of the US was under constant consideration during 1944 until we find Edward Turner writing again to Bill Johnson with a letter dated 13 October of that year.]

We are in receipt of your cable of the 8th inst which reads:

YOUR DECISION ON OUR BEHALF IS ACCEPTED WITH GREAT PLEASURE AND APPRECIATION STOP REST ASSURED THAT YOUR INTERESTS WILL ALWAYS RECEIVE OUR BEST EFFORTS.

and which was in answer to our cable of 5th inst reading as follows:

REFERENCE YOUR LETTER 21 SEPTEMBER HAVE PLEASURE IN ACCEDING TO YOUR REQUEST FOR OPPORTUNITY EXPLOIT ENTIRE USA LETTER FOLLOWS.

It will be as well for us to review the situation leading up to this exchange of cables. When Child offered his services to us we were impressed by his successful record in the motor cycle industry and we came to the conclusion that he would undoubtedly make a success of the sale of our machines in the Eastern States. Bearing in mind your excellent record with us and the cordial basis on which we have been able to do business in the past, we feel obliged to give you the opportunity of exploiting the nationwide territory, since you have expressed this desire. Therefore it can be taken that we agree this in principle.

It is desirable that we appreciate at the outset the magnitude of this policy. For instance, in Australia we have five distributors who sold from 800–1,000 machines annually in a country with a population of eight million people. The US has a population of 135,000,000 – seventeen times as great – and, making all allowances for its own domestic manufacture of two very important firms, the competition from our own country, which, I understand, is going to be keen, and the different psychology of the population (less motor cycle minded), it does not seem unreasonable to me to expect that, within twelve months, the US could take at least 1,000 motor cycles annually from Triumph, and, thereafter, when the motorcycling movement based on our own lighter and more efficient machines gains impetus, sales will soar until the US market should be good for many thousands of Triumph machines.

If you agree with this, you may perhaps not regard it as unreasonable if we reserve the right to review our arrangements with you after, say, two years from the time when deliveries commence, when, if we are satisfied that we are getting a reasonable share of the motorcycle market, we should renew our agreement as a matter of course. At this moment there are so many unknown factors in the situation, such as our own prices, the tariff position, cost of freight charges, that it would be impossible to arrive at a mutually satisfactory basis on which you are to act virtually as our factory representative for the whole territory, but we can at this stage say that we should expect you to open an office and warehouse on the Eastern side to carry on this business. Next we should expect the appointment of distributors in most of the important States, who, in turn, are big enough to attract smaller agents in the various towns.

We understand our British competitors are keen on a large number of independent distributors, but we feel, with the lead that Triumph has established, that, providing you tackle the situation on broad lines and do not expect too high a margin in your capacity as key distributors, the British competition need not be very serious. In any case you will not be asked to finance the consignments as Scholefield Goodman & Sons Ltd will doubtless be very pleased to participate in the opening up of this market with us.

We naturally want you to make a good thing out of these possibilities, but, at the same time, we wish to see our products on the American market at the lowest prices in relation to landed cost that is compatible with all the circumstances prevailing at the time. It will probably be much more satisfactory to you if, between now and the delivery of new machines, we enter into an agreement covering all points concerned with the marketing of our goods in America, so that we each know where we stand and this will be done as soon as the situation clarifies in regard to prices, the tariff position, etc.

It seems clear, however, that if you are to tackle the nationwide distribution of Triumph machines you will virtually have two separate businesses, that of your own retail organization in California, and the other as a sales promotion enterprise linked with it but operating differently. After the war we are told that Britain will have to export more, and that the US will have to accept goods from debtor nations, since she already has most of the world's gold.

I believe that motor cycles, in a small way, are one of the commodities that America can buy in sufficient quantities to amount to considerable business, but without seriously damaging its domestic industry and, from our point of view, the US will assume as an export market, a very considerably more important position in relation to our other export markets than has been the case hitherto.

From evidence that we are continually receiving in the form of letters from dealers, enthusiasts and even soldiers stationed over here, strengthens our belief in the fact that our twin cylinder types are exactly what the American market wants, and, although other British manufacturers will, by then, have twin-cylinder machines to offer, the advantage lies with us in as much as ours is a tried and proven product – *and we are not asleep!*

Please, therefore, give this situation your consideration and we shall await your comments with interest.

Reply from Bill Johnson Jnr

9 November 1944

The proposition outlined generally in your letter of 18 October impresses us as being eminently reasonable. We appreciate that your decision to appoint us as your United States distributors and factory representatives was made only after considerable thought, as now the United States is recognized as being probably your most important post-war market. The magnitude of this policy is well understood and you have our assurance that the interests of Triumph will be handled in a sound, straightforward manner which we know will meet with your entire satisfaction. We are therefore very enthusiastic in accepting the appointment.

Your reservation to review the arrangement after two years of business is entirely acceptable to us and we also share the view that a written agreement covering all points concerned with the distribution of your goods is desirable, as it will give us a mutual understanding of what is expected when trade can be resumed.

At present it is impossible to anticipate such factors as your manufacturing costs, tariffs, freight etc. However, we are in accord with you in principle, that we as your factory representatives should undertake the job on broad lines and not expect too high a margin in our capacity as distributors. I am sure that a mutually satisfactory arrangement can be agreed upon, and after trade is resumed and our dealer organization is firmly established, we would be amenable to reducing our margin as distributors, if at the time the circumstances warrant it. As you have mentioned, our retail business in California will be related to our sales promotion program, although they will be two separate businesses.

Speaking of local matters, Vard Inc of Pasadena are considering the manufacture of a medium price ($300) 350cc side-valve single-cylinder motorcycle. It is not certain that they will actually undertake such a proposition. While Vard has a small well equipped plant, they are primarily engaged in the manufacture of drafting instruments, gauges etc, and their facilities for the most part are intended for that use. The manufacture of motorcycles in sufficient volume to make the venture worthwhile will require the investment of considerable capital in additional plant facilities. I doubt if they are prepared to do this; however, I mention the plan as Vard has indicated that they would perhaps prefer to turn over the sales of their machine to us and not become involved in this aspect of the business . . . it might be to our advantage to handle the sales rather than our competitors. Would like your comments.

Meriden Gets Down to Work

Right through Edward Turner's letters to Bill Johnson was the recurring theme of post-war business. To him, the war had become a nuisance which was causing serious delays to legitimate business. He did not promise any startling

Ted Crabtree and Eddie Gough

In the Buying Office, Ted Crabtree was in charge, assisted by Eddie Gough. Ted later moved to Ariel as General Manager and Eddie took over at Triumph. He was a popular member of staff and was reckoned to be the sharpest buyer in the industry. He kept the tracks rolling for many years and made a major contribution to the profitability of the company. Crabtree was sadly killed in a car crash some years later.

new models immediately, but was confident that Triumph would soon get into top gear again. Bikes would start to flow out of the works to the markets of the world and particularly to America, which Turner saw as the number one market – and how right he was! Before the war, Turner had realized that America was a market waiting to be created – its young men were the same sporting young men to be found everywhere else, but they had not been exposed to motorcycling as we knew it. Their domestic manufacturers, just two in all, had been producing the same big clumsy machines for thirty years or more and the only customers they had, of any consequence, were the police.

As Turner said in one letter, Harley Davidson and Indian were more concerned in doing each other down than in developing new models and new markets. Bill Johnson was particularly successful in introducing his cus-

tomers to the joys of riding motorcycles which did not weigh a ton and which could be handled easily (you did not have to be a 6ft-6in-220lb cop) – they were also exceedingly fast.

To give some idea of how Meriden did get into gear after the war, I have some production figures for the immediate post-war period. It should be borne in mind that these figures were achieved in the face of enormous difficulties. Everything was in short supply – metals, rubber, machine tools, electrics – delays were an everyday occurrence. The Buying Department under Ted Crabtree and Eddie Gough had a hard life chasing every single item that went to make up a motorcycle – their lives were spent on the phone to suppliers. How well they did can be seen from the following figures:

YEAR	TOTAL OUTPUT	EXPORT PERCENTAGE
1946	9,477	44.4%
1947	10,000	54%
1948	11,841	67%
1949	11,877	63.5%
1950	14,306	66%
1951 (to 4 May)	5,065	64.7%
TOTAL	62,566	**AVERAGE** 60%

Turner on America

In 1945 Edward Turner paid his first visit to the US since before the war. On his return, he wrote this report:

4 October 1945

The purpose of my visit to the US was to survey the possibilities of motor cycle exports to that country, which were promising before the war as far as Triumph machines were concerned, and to arrange for efficient distribution throughout the United States.

On landing at New York after a fast voyage in one of our latest single-engine diesel freighters in eight days, I flew by night plane to Chicago and thereafter by normal lines to the West Coast (Los Angeles).

One was struck by the efficiency and smoothness of the organization of American airlines, which have now arrived at fast travel facilities cheaper than first class travel in the US. These airlines must be of enormous benefit to the American business man, as one of the disadvantages normally of a vast country like the US is the distances, and airlines have now reduced these distances on a time basis to those equivalent in this country; in other words one can practically fly from coast to coast at a moderate fare in approximately the same time as it takes from London to Glasgow.

Motor cycles have for many years in the US been the hobby of the few, the principal industry being maintained on Police machines. However, the few hundreds we sent before the war indicated a new interest in motorcycling by a certain type of young man who was moderately well off. He preferred a well-made English Triumph machine with its sparkling performance to the heavy American big twin, which is all that remains of the many US types developed over the years.

California, of course, and many other states in America are ideal for motorcycling owing to the excellent climate, where there is sunshine more often than not, and when weather is bad it is predictable within narrow limits.

Cars in America have long since become a means of transport rather than a sport, and it is estimated that a large proportion of the young men of the fighting forces of the US will take up motorcycling as a hobby and as a means of getting about the country. This offers a first class opportunity for British manufacturers under present conditions, but eventually America will develop her own machines on British lines, as indicated by several prototypes inspected by me in Los Angeles alone, all of which closely follow British trends.

Coming back from war-time US to war-time Britain, one is struck by the innumerable restrictions still imposed upon our people and one cannot help feeling that the time is now overdue when a little more liberty and easement should be granted to the sorely tried people of Britain. A little more petrol, a little more variety in food, and a little more travel facility would, I feel sure, not only be most welcome but, no one can deny, has been well and truly earned. In America the ordinary people experience very

Generator set developed for the RAF using a Triumph 500cc twin engine with an alloy head and barrel.

little restriction as far as I could see; life is just as pleasant for them as it was . . . in 1939, and certainly one notices the difference in the demeanour of the people.

It will be necessary for more business men to visit the US as the balance of economic forces has changed very considerably as a result of the war, and it is impossible for any British business man to evaluate these forces until he has seen the colossal development of the US industrial market.

I do not know what the British airlines are doing but I am given to understand that in 1946 TWA American Air Lines will be running a service of Lockheed Constellations, cruising at 300 miles an hour [480kph] between Britain and America. This will enable a business man to be in San Francisco from London in twenty-three hours, with a high degree of comfort and, thanks to war-time development, a high degree of safety. Every advantage should be taken of

this, as it will be more necessary than ever in the future for Britain to link up her trading policy with that of America.

One sensed that the US is very sympathetic towards this country and emotionally disturbed with our losses and hardships, but when it comes to big business, there will be no quarter and we must really work as we have never worked before, both management and workpeople, to maintain even the standard of living we enjoyed in 1937/1938. By doing this and with a further development in collaboration with our Dominions it will be possible to keep our end up. If we fail, I see no hope for Britain but that of sinking into a pitiable state of shabby genteel respectability.

Things have moved on a little since 1945 with Concorde cruising at 1,300 miles an hour and getting to America in about three hours, ET would have loved every minute!

The Triumph Corporation

Although we have seen from the correspondence that it was Edward Turner's original intention that Johnson Motors Inc of Pasadena, California, should take over the marketing of Triumph motorcycles for the whole of the United States, he soon became convinced that the sales potential of the eastern side of that vast country was enormous and would require specialist treatment. At this time, Johnson Motors were doing very nicely, importing around 1,000 machines a year, so plans were laid to set up an entirely new organization to look after the eastern half.

Turner consulted an old friend and two-wheel enthusiast, Percival White, President of the Market Research Corporation of America. White, after some investigation, agreed with Turner that there could be a very good market for British type motor cycles in the eastern States.

Turner and McCormack alongside the plaque commemorating the opening of the Baltimore headquarters of the Triumph Corporation, a wholly-owned subsidiary of Meriden.

So, the Triumph Corporation came into being in 1951, as a wholly-owned subsidiary of the Meriden factory. It was based in Baltimore and headed by Denis McCormack, who was Percival White's Vice-President in charge of European accounts. It was a happy coincidence that McCormack was an expatriate Englishman born in Coventry. After working with several companies in the automotive industry there, and also in Birmingham, he moved to America. Percival White agreed, following a meeting with Sangster and Turner, that McCormack should move into this new organization as President. Denis McCormack was a very interesting man, and a man of many interests, and we always enjoyed his visits to Meriden. He made a great success of the Corporation.

Don Brown, Senior Marketing and Sales Executive for nearly ten years with the Johnson organization on the West Coast explains what happened next:

McCormack, working from scratch, rapidly built up the nucleus of a staff who served him well for many years. Earl Miller, an astute accountant, Rod Coates, Service Manager and one-time winner of the Daytona 100 race on a Triumph, Jack Mercer, roadman extraordinary, Phillis Fansler, Office Organizer who had been at Bendix with McCormack, finally John Wright, lawyer, to steer the new company through the legal jungles. Johnson was not entirely happy about this new arrangement but was obliged to agree, since the promotion and servicing of sales in a country the size of the United States would require more capital than he was willing or able to risk. It was not a

In the early sixties, the Triumph Corporation of Baltimore added Daimler cars to their portfolio. Here we see Denis McCormack (President), Edward Turner, Earl Miller (Chief Accountant) and Jack Wickes at the Baltimore location.

happy decision either for Edward Turner, but he was convinced, as was Jack Sangster, that dividing up the country would benefit all concerned in the long term. As subsequent events would confirm, he was absolutely right.

American Shipments

To give some idea of the American market which Edward Turner, Bill Johnson and Denis McCormack built up out of nothing, I give below some figures of shipments to East and West Coasts for the years 1958 to 1965 and their value in monetary terms:

YEAR	JOHNSON MOTORS INC (West)	TRIUMPH CORPORATION (East)
1958	1,756	2,797
1959	2,458	3,267
1960	2,787	3,799
1961	1,009	1,478
1962	2,047	2,460
1963	3,378	4,295
1964	4,773	4,802
1965	6,531	8,807
Total	24,739	31,705
Value	£1,324,803	£1,888,692
Spares	£115,077	£174,081
Total	£1,439,880	£2,062,773
Total Value Motorcycles shipped (No of MC/s 56,444)		£3,213,495
Total Value Spares shipped		289,158
Grand Total		£3,502,653

The Triumph Corporation had to work in more or less virgin territory for Triumph in the east. To add to their problems, Harley Davidson, furious that their comfortable monopoly was being challenged, and by foreign interests at that, had placed pressure on their dealers not to handle Triumph or any other brand. The result of this was that McCormack had to look around for entirely new people and found many of them in the ex-servicemen seeking some way to invest their gratuities. He also picked up some Indian dealers, that once great company having all but expired. Training schools were held to teach not only Triumph service and repair work, but also the basics of running a business – finance, stocking, promotion, etc. Johnson Motors set up the same procedures in the west and it became an annual routine for Edward Turner and senior personnel from the factory to attend these schools to back up the local instructors and dispense the latest information from headquarters.

10

Post-War Motorcycle Development

In April 1943 Edward Turner was asked by The Institution of Automobile Engineers to place on record his thoughts and views on post-war motorcycle development. I was shown a copy of this recently and immediately felt it should have a place in this book, although what follows is not the complete paper but my own brief summaries and extracts from the sections I judged to be of greatest interest.

Turner starts by criticising the industry for failing to expand, notwithstanding the vastly improved roads throughout the UK plus the constant need of the community to use independent transport. He hoped that his suggestions for future designs would help to provide better machines that would appeal to a broader market. He outlined the specification of the typical current motorcycle as having a single-cylinder pushrod OHV engine with a separate four-speed gearbox with positive-stop foot change. The frame was tubular steel jointed by brazed lugs. Transmission was by chain from engine to gearbox and from gearbox to rear wheel. Wheels were wire-spoked with 26 x 3.25in tyres.

Sport, i.e. road racing and trials, provided a stimulus for designers and valuable copy for the technical journals. The latter had done much good over the years by promoting discussion on improvements to design and been successful in encouraging many beneficial changes. Nevertheless he was sure that the trend of development in recent years had been in the wrong direction and had tended to narrow the scope of appeal of the motorcycle.

Aiming at a considerable enlargement of the market, ET outlined requirements in design to achieve this. The machine of the future he suggested should:

1. Be economical to buy and use.
2. Have good weather protection.
3. Be as silent as possible.
4. Be easy to start and idle with certainty.
5. Be easy to clean and maintain, with enclosed 'works'.

6. Be as reliable as the average car.
7. Be easy to handle, less vulnerable and have maximum stability.

Then followed extensive comments on the various types of motorcycle engine and their advantages and disadvantages – whether singles, vertical twins, V-twins, horizontally-opposed twins, straight fours, four-in-line, V-fours, horizontally-opposed fours, etc.

On the subject of vertical twins, about which he was undoubtedly *the* authority (!) he said:

Parallel twin would be more apt as the cylinders are parallel with each other and the connecting rods are mounted on a single throw crankshaft so that they move together. This arrangement in a four-stroke engine gives good torque, but poor balance as compared with a similar twin that has a two-throw crankshaft with cranks at 180deg. The balance, however, is superior to that of a single of equal capacity, whereas the torque of the 180deg version is poor, and causes carburation difficulties.

Everyone who has ever wondered why Triumph pistons go up and down together instead of alternately, now have their answer – from the master himself!

Moving on to gearboxes, he classed them as generally reliable but considered four speeds to be an unnecessary luxury for utility machines and forecasted a return to three. The general design of the gearbox was unlikely to change, but the necessity to move the gearbox bodily to take up the slack in a chain was 'unforgiveable'. He also pointed out that the slack in a straight-sided link chain could now be taken up by an adjustable slipper or skate, copiously lubricated as it was, in an oilbath chaincase. This enabled the gears to be embodied in the crankcase casting, saving weight and damping out vibration. This is precisely what happened at Triumph in 1958 with the Twenty-One and the bigger twins from 1964. Turner dismissed shaft drive for his utility model as too costly, but advocated a pressed-steel frame as being cheaper to produce, despite high tool charges. It was also cleaner in appearance, just as reliable, and more attractive in shape.

On suspension, he reckoned that the girder fork had served the industry well, being economical to produce, not critical of accuracy in manufacture and if bent in a minor bump, the machine could still be ridden. However it called for frequent adjustment and lubrication and deteriorated rapidly if neglected. The telescopic fork had come to stay for high performance machines as it offered better shock-absorbing qualities and larger effective movement. It was too expensive for low price models though.

Rear suspension was a 'long-felt need' on high power machines, mainly to provide better roadholding (and therefore safety) rather than comfort. Here again he felt that in its present form it was expensive and complicated and would not warrant the extra cost on utility motorcycles. He goes on to say that, 'a sound, inexpensive resilient device either in the frame or rear wheel' could be a worthwhile improvement. The Triumph Spring Wheel must have been in his mind even then – it was announced in 1947. Normal, wire-spoked wheels would remain basically unaltered 'for many years to come'. No thoughts on pressed-steel wheels at all – I am sure that the very ugly specimens one sees around today would have found no place on Turner's drawing board.

Electrical equipment comes in for a hammering but the vibration and exposure to which it was subjected was appreciated. Coil ignition was likely to be used more and more on the basis of cost and simplicity, but 'that necessary evil', the battery, he regarded as small and overstressed in comparison with its car counterpart. Wiring layouts would have to be improved as failures were common. Direct lighting would suffice for the low-price machine. Electric starting he classed as 'over development of the simple motorcycle'. . . Tell that to the Japanese!

Carburettors got a good word as being reliable, easily understood and adjusted – but unnecessarily expensive and heavy on fuel. A utility motorcycle weighing under 200lb (90kg) and capable of 55mph (90kph) should give 200mpg (70km per litre)!

Weight would be saved (and therefore cost) if the price gap between steel and aluminium was to be reduced as a result of the war. A long list of components could be beneficially made of light alloy – cylinder heads, cylinders, connecting rods, hubs, rims, clutch plates, brake anchor plates, saddle frames, mudguards, petrol and oil tanks. These components had been well developed already for trials and racing and the degree of price reduction of light alloys would determine the extent to which they would be used in the future. With the extensive use of light alloys, a

A happy ceremony to celebrate the 400,000th British motorcycle made during the war. It was not necessarily a Triumph, the manufacturers drew lots as to where the ceremony should be held and Triumph won! Edward Turner is talking to Jack Welton. Alf Camwell, Works Director, is standing between the two military figures.

weight reduction could be made in the steel parts, thus effecting a further saving in weight.

Plastics would appear to have a future, but in their present stage of development and cost it was doubtful if they could be used with much advantage in motorcycle construction.

On the subject of general appearance, Turner stated that all other things being equal, the customer would go for the better-looking commodity. For motorcycles the designer must: 'a) Get his mechanism to work, b) Make it reliable, c) Make it cheap and d) Make it beautiful'. The last two processes did not conflict; good shape was not more costly.

Good shape was something that all Edward Turner's products had in abundance – he was a master at it and a lot of the success of his designs can be put down to the way they looked – they also functioned very well of course. Every component, large and small, was designed to look good and Jack Wickes, Turner's 'pencil', was brilliant in finalising ET's concepts on the drawing board.

The Future

Turner's view of the motorcycle industry after the war was that it should concentrate on five types of motorcycle:

1. Power-assisted bicycle up to 100cc.
2. Primary motorcycle up to 150cc.
3. Utility or touring motorcycle 250/350cc.
4. Light sports motorcycle 350cc.
5. High performance motorcycle 500/1,000cc.

These categories would provide a 'broad field for the industry to plan for and with ingenuity, enterprise and courage could greatly enlarge the scope of the industry and make it a real national asset in our participation in world trade'.

Discussion

The discussion that followed this peroration at the Institution was led by Arthur Bourne, famed Editor of *The Motor Cycle*, who pointed out that although Edward Turner had dismissed shaft drive for low-price models on the grounds of cost, he had not commented on it in relation to the more expensive models. Whatever form the final transmission took – whether it be belt, chain or shaft – it must be clean and trouble-free in use. This was not the case at present where the rear chain of a spring-frame machine never lasted more than a mere 7,000 or 8,000 miles (11,300 or 12,900km). Did Mr Turner consider that it was possible and preferable so to enclose the rear chain of a fully-sprung machine that it was in every way satisfactory?

Other points Mr Bourne raised concerned girder forks on cheap machines (which Mr Turner appeared to favour) with their multiplicity of links and bearing surfaces which were inadequate laterally, and their habit of exuding vile black grease. Then there was the need for accessibility – essential maintenance took far too long. Also, the necessity for a big reduction in the absurdly large number of nut and bolt sizes as well as the standardization of screw threads.

In Conclusion

It is odd that Edward Turner, all through his talk, emphasized his interest in the 'utility' motorcycle. As long as I can remember, the industry has had this vision of vast numbers of the population 'out there' who are just waiting to jump on this wonderful 'utility' motorcycle when someone has made it. The notorious Ariel 3 was designed entirely with this market in mind, as was the LE Velocette. Where are they now?

When business resumed after the war the only 'utility' machine from the Turner board was the Triumph 3TU, which did not get past the single-prototype stage. It was an odd little machine, unlike anything else from Meriden. It had a 350cc twin engine with vertical valves operated by pushrods from a single camshaft behind the block. Cylinders were cast in one with the upper half of the horizontally-split crankcase. The gearbox had three speeds, the frame was rigid and had undamped telescopic forks. The wheels were pressed-steel 'discs' and mudguarding was voluminous. So, although Turner showed interest in this utility market, the 3TU disappeared and Meriden went on turning out high-performance twins for which the customers were waiting, and the profits high!

11

Turner is Back

Edward Turner returned to Triumph in late 1943 as Managing Director and soon got to work on the post-war range, which was announced towards the end of 1945. This comprised the Speed Twin, Tiger 100 and the new 350cc twin, the 3T de Luxe. The latter was all set to be

The war is over and here is the Speed Twin in 1946-guise, with a four-gallon tank and telescopic forks.

announced when war broke out, but had to be postponed. The single-cylinder 3H was also included, but was never actually made, so the range was an all-twin-cylinder one.

Basically, the models were the same as pre-war with two major alterations. The girder fork had gone, to be replaced by a telescopic fork of Triumph design. Rear springing was offered as an extra by the ingenious patented Spring Wheel. This did provide a limited amount of movement, but could not be compared with the much superior swinging-arm system adopted later.

It was at this point that I joined the company. Just pre-war when I was working for a major advertising agency in London, the department I was in closed down possibly because of the war scare and I was temporarily out of a job. I had a short spell as a motorcycle runner for a Fleet Street photographer and then decided to try to combine pleasure with business and wrote to Edward Turner offering my services. I was invited to Coventry and interviewed by the great man himself.

To my surprise, shortly after, I was invited to join the company as Publicity Manager. However, Hitler interve-

Near-side view of the 1946 Speed Twin, a handsome motorcycle by any reckoning.

ned, war broke out and being a Territorial I was in it from Day One.

Six years later, in Burma, when the Japanese were on the point of giving up, I wrote to Meriden reminding them of their offer. Back came a reply from Jack Welton asking me to contact them directly I was demobbed. This I did and after another interview with Turner and, this time, a

chat with Charles Parker, the job was mine. I started on the first day of January 1946 which was an easy date to remember ever after.

The original interview in 1939 was at Priory Street and the second at Meriden in 1946 – both journeys from London being on the same bike, my faithful old six-stud Speed Twin which had burst into song almost first kick

C W F Parker, Financial Director and Secretary of the Triumph Engineering Co Ltd.

Charles William Fenning Parker

Charles Parker was the Financial Director and Secretary who jealously guarded the finances of the company to the very end and made such a good job of it that he never failed to show a resounding profit! He was a trained accountant obviously, but in the days before the war he was for a time on the Birmingham staff of *Motor Cycling* magazine where he handled road tests and generally acted for that journal. Just how he came to Edward Turner's notice is not known, but it was a lucky day for Triumph when he joined. He was very popular and held in great respect by everyone. You could always go to him with a problem because he had that unique ability to sort it out so easily that afterwards you wondered why you had bothered him. He was a railway enthusiast like myself and with business done we would often discuss the genius of G J Churchward, Chief Mechanical Engineer of the Great Western Railway and ponder whether the latter's remarkable loco component standardization scheme could be applied with advantage to the motorcycle industry. Parker's very able secretary, Brenda Price, worked with him for many years.

after sitting in its shed for four years while I was away. The clutch plates did take some separating though!

Back to Work

After six years in the army travelling the world it was strange to get back to a civilian existence again – nine to five and no night shifts! If you had been in the forces, Alec Masters, Service Manager, was always keen to do what he could to help you settle in. He had been in the forces himself and knew the problems. He located some nice digs for me in Kenilworth and I settled in very comfortably. As far as the work was concerned, I was somewhat rusty after so many years away, but soon got into the swing again. The pressure was not as high at Meriden as it had been in London. Advertising was confined to the two weekly journals *Motor Cycling* and *The Motor Cycle*, and the trade paper *Cycle Trader*. We had an advertising agent in Birmingham and between us we came up with schemes

Jack Welton

Jack Welton was another old hand at Triumph, in UK Sales, in the days before the war. Like Alf Camwell, he was a staunch Coventrian – his father being a well known butcher in the city. When Turner arrived on the scene at Priory Street and started sorting out the organization, Jack Welton was made manager of the sales department, not Sales Manager, note. His job was administrative, keeping records of motorcycle dispatches, dealing with salesmen's reports, keeping dealers happy and generally acting as liaison officer between the sales force out in the country and the works. I had a lot to do with Jack, as publicity and sales operated in very close harmony, particularly at the annual Earls Court shows in London, and he was a very conscientious man and very loyal to Triumph where he had worked since Bettmann days.

Twin-cylinder engine (350cc) for the new 3T de Luxe. It was developed from the aborted 3TW Services model, so that frustrating experience was not wasted in the end.

The Tiger 85 of 1946. Intended as a sporting version of the new 350cc 3T de Luxe, it was in the catalogue but was not produced.

that seemed to please Edward Turner – at least he did not throw them out too often!

I was not used to life in a factory and it took a little time to get acclimatized. It was a fascinating place, though, and I used to watch enthralled as the machines in the Machine Shop drilled and milled and cut their way through the metal to produce the familiar crankcases, gear wheels and other components with which I was familiar in their finished state. The Machine Shop had a rather 'olde worlde' look about it, as most of the machines were driven by overhead belting. With the war barely over, it was almost impossible to get brand new machine tools and most of those at Meriden had been recovered from the blitzed factory at Priory Street, which was largely belt-driven, like so many of the motorcycles it had made. The operatives were a very friendly bunch, always ready to explain exactly what they were doing. I usually asked them because one of my jobs was showing important visitors round the works. It was nice to be able to show off by explaining what was happening at each machine – as long as the visitor did not start asking too many technical questions!

Another view of the Tiger 85, a pretty little bike.

A thinly-disguised works-prepared Tiger 100 won the 1946 Manx Grand Prix in the hands of Irishman Ernie Lyons. A small batch of replicas of the Lyons machine was then produced for sale. This is one of them.

Apart from starting work at Meriden, another exciting thing that happened in 1946 was in the Isle of Man, where Ernie Lyons won the Manx Grand Prix on a Tiger 100, defeating a galaxy of Nortons, much to their owners' surprise and dismay! The Lyons machine had been prepared by Freddie Clarke and was undoubtedly a flyer, but its ultimate performance was not called on as the weather was appalling. The rain bucketed down all through. How Lyons even saw where he was going without trying to win a race, was beyond me. I will not go into the details of this race as it has been told many times, but I was involved at the end when we saw that the Tiger 100 had broken its front down tube just above the engine plates and we had some fun preventing the press getting at it with cameras.

In 1947 Bert Hopwood left Triumph to join Norton as Chief Designer. Their model range was very long in the tooth, very noisy mechanically and not very appealing in the showroom. Hopwood's first job was to design a new twin, named the Dominator which became the forerunner of a number of impressive twin-cylinder models which added lustre to Norton's tarnished image. Needless to say we were all very sorry to see him go and delighted when he came back again in 1961, but that is another part of the story which comes later.

12

New Models

The New Look

When the 1949 range was announced, it was seen that Turner and Wickes had decided to clean up that notoriously untidy area of every motorcycle: around the headlamp. From the very early days, the headlamp had been regarded as an 'extra' and was tacked on to the front of the machine with the aid of two little brackets sticking out from the forks. Of course, it remained in fact, an 'extra' for a very long time and the customer had to specify if he wanted it, and if he did, he had to pay accordingly. This was a hangover from pedal-cycle days and it lasted a long time. The car world followed the same route – headlamps were mounted on brackets more or less as an afterthought and it was only much later that they were enclosed in the body shell.

The 1949 models from Meriden struck a completely new note. The headlamp was incorporated in the top end of the telescopic forks in a very shapely nacelle, which also took in the speedometer, the ammeter, the light switch, cut-out button and steering-damper knob. It looked very attractive and was an absolutely unique Triumph feature – one by which the make could be instantly recognized. It was also easy to clean.

There were three models only in the range at this time, the 350cc 3T de Luxe, the 500cc Speed Twin and the Tiger 100, and all now carried the nacelle.

The following year, another unique feature came out, the very useful tank-top parcel grid which was chromium-plated and brightened up the top of the tank from which the chrome panels had now been eliminated.

The classic Triumph 'look' was finalized in these years and it did not change very much in the years that followed. Everything looked right and it reflects great credit on Turner, who was a master of shapes and Jack Wickes, who could and did translate them from Turner's concepts into the real thing. No detail was too small. Look at the front number plate of the period with its flowing lines and chrome edging, the rear number plate with its totally illegal curved surface, the timing cover specially shaped around the screw heads (like mouse's ears, someone said) and so on – it was a beautiful total look and many other

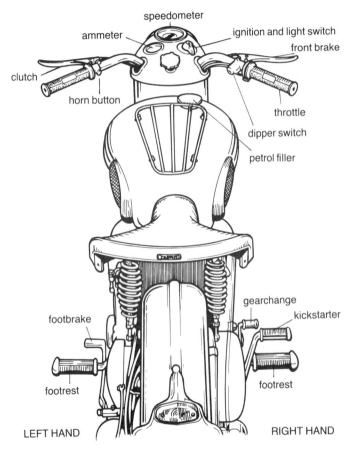

speedometer

ammeter   ignition and light switch

front brake

clutch

horn button

throttle

dipper switch

petrol filler

footbrake

gearchange

kickstarter

footrest

footrest

LEFT HAND   RIGHT HAND

Control layout of twin cylinder models fitted with the unique and very stylish Triumph nacelle headlamp arrangement introduced in 1949.

manufacturers sought to copy it (including some very prominent companies not based in this country).

Years later, when the three-cylinder Trident was being developed, outside stylists from the car industry were engaged to give it a space-age appearance. The machine went into production with its slab-sided tank, as opposed to the traditional bulbous one and was immediately rejected by the Americans – they said it 'was not a Triumph', and I think they were right. At any rate, a new tank was produced which was more in the Triumph tradition and everyone was happy again. It does show how important good styling is – it can affect the company bank balance very seriously.

The Trophy Model

This model, introduced in 1948, achieved great popularity over the next few years.

The name originated in the ISDT of that year. Alan Jefferies and Jim Alves had been selected as members of the official British team competing for the International Trophy, the top award in the trial. Alan captained the team which was successful in winning the Trophy, all members retaining clean sheets. The machines used by the Triumph riders were much-modified Speed Twins which used the alloy head and barrel from the wartime generator set to save weight. They also featured in the Tiger 100 of Ernie Lyons, which won the 1946 Manx Grand Prix, and subsequently incorporated in the production Grand Prix models.

Jack Wickes

In the drawing office there was Jack Wickes, draughtsman, artist, stylist. He started at Priory Street in 1931 at the age of sixteen as a print boy, delivering blueprints around the works. His father was the Despatch Manager who thought that young Jack's undoubted artistic talents could best be employed in the Triumph Drawing Office. How right he was, as we shall see. When the company was in trouble in 1936, and it became known that Jack Sangster was taking over, Wickes decided to stay. He liked the look of Sangster and Turner and what was more, they had offered him a job with an increase! He was then twenty-one. Turner soon took to him – Wickes's knowledge of the Priory Street set-up was invaluable to Turner and from there he progressed to being Turner's Personal Assistant on the design side. Over the next forty years he was responsible for putting the finishing touches to Turner's concepts which resulted in Triumph producing the best-looking British motorcycles of all time. Turner once said of him: 'Oh yes, young Wickes – he's my pencil.'

Jack Wickes, engineer, stylist, artist and PA to Edward Turner through all those post-war years.

After the trial, it was decided that the ISDT machine might form the basis of a good sports model which could be used for everyday road work as well as competitions. The Speed Twin basis was discarded as being too heavy, but the engine with its alloy head and barrel was retained. The result was the Trophy, a light, quick 500 which handled well and soon became a firm favourite.

The Thunderbird Model

This model was launched the following year and was evolved to meet the cry from America for more power. It was a simple bore-and-stroke job to increase the 63 x 80mm (498cc) engine to 71 x 82mm (649cc). The rest of the specification remained unchanged.

Another post-war model that never saw the light of day. It was probably a 550cc side-valve in the best Triumph tradition, going back to the 1915 model H.

Trophy model, 1949 – a beautiful little bike with an all-alloy engine. Worth a fortune today!

*Thunderbird model, 1949, 650cc – first of the
Superbikes! It achieved 100mph (160kph)
performance at a reasonable price. It was a winner.*

*The unique Triumph nacelle which came with the
Thunderbird and was applied to all models thereafter.
It tidied up the most untidy area to be found on the
motorcycle.*

The Thunderbird was launched in fine style with a demonstration of speed and reliability which has been described many times. Very briefly, three standard production models were ridden to the Montlhéry circuit near Paris where, in the hands of a team of riders, they each covered 500 miles at 92mph (800km at 148kph) with terminal laps at more than 100mph (160km). They were then ridden back to Meriden.

This performance gained wide publicity and the success of the 650cc engine in future years and in a wide range of models was assured.

Some years later, the name 'Thunderbird' having been well established and also registered as a trade name in the US, the Ford car people put it about that they were going to use this name for a new sports car. Their attention was directed to the fact that the name had been used and widely advertised as applying to a Triumph motorcycle.

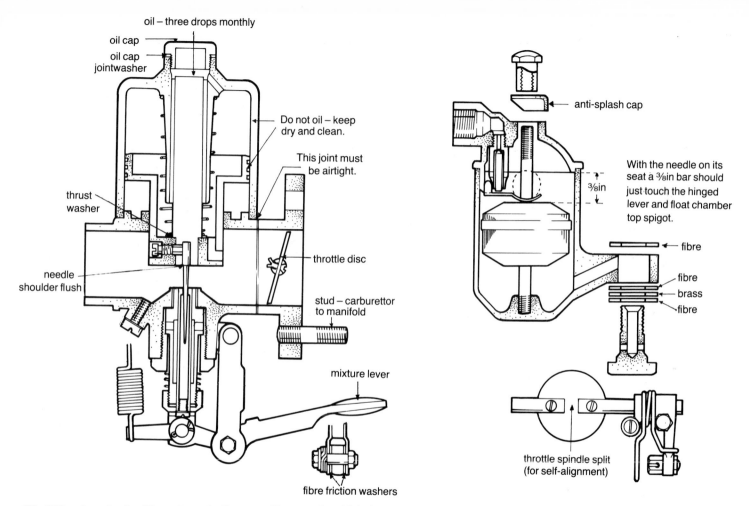

oil – three drops monthly

oil cap

oil cap jointwasher

Do not oil – keep dry and clean.

This joint must be airtight.

thrust washer

needle shoulder flush

throttle disc

stud – carburettor to manifold

mixture lever

fibre friction washers

anti-splash cap

With the needle on its seat a ⅜in bar should just touch the hinged lever and float chamber top spigot.

⅜in

fibre

fibre

brass

fibre

throttle spindle split (for self-alignment)

The SU carburettor is of the automatically-expanding type, in which the cross-sectional area of the air passage and the effective orifice of the jet are variable. It was fitted to the Triumph 650cc Thunderbird from 1953–1958 and provided good performance with exceptional economy.

Percy Tait and Alex Scobie

These testers were two of the hardest riders in the business. Both were employed to test to destruction, if possible, anything new that came out of the Experimental Department. They covered vast mileages, day in, day out, in fair weather or foul, and loved it! Percy, of course, was a racer in his spare time, well known on all the circuits and his successes were numerous. Alex had also raced in his earlier days up north before coming to Meriden. He was one of the team of riders in the Thunderbird Montlhéry demonstration in 1949. I am sorry to have to report that Alex died in August 1990 whilst this book was being written.

They replied, very courteously, that their understanding was that the name had been registered to apply to a 'two-wheeled vehicle' and by applying it to a four-wheeled vehicle, there would be no legal infringement. They said that they would make every effort not to 'tarnish the high reputation' which they understood we had earned in the use of the name!

The Tiger 110

Following his usual procedure of introducing a new model followed later by a sports version (e.g. Speed Twin/Tiger 100) Turner did the same with the Thunderbird. Here the sports version was the Tiger 110 introduced in 1954. High compression pistons (8.5:1), special camshafts, large bore carburettor, new, heavier crankshaft etc, all combined to produce an even higher performance from the already very quick Thunderbird.

Triumph's Baby – The Terrier

In 1953, Edward Turner added a real Triumph lightweight to the range – something which had not been seen in the Triumph catalogue for a very long time: 1913 was the first occasion on which the 'Junior' 225cc two-stroke was launched in November of that year. Next, in 1933, came two Villiers-engined lightweights (98cc and 147cc) costing £16.16s and £21 respectively, produced to take advantage of a 15/- tax rate introduced on 1 January 1933 for engines under 150cc. These were followed very quickly by two Triumph-engined 147cc OHV singles, fitted into the two-stroke frame. These were the XO5/1 and the XO5/5, the latter a sporting version with upswept pipe. The engines were slopers and the fins ran parallel to the ground.

Back to 1953 (strange how these babies crop up in 1913, 1933 and 1953). Turner's lightweight was also a sloping 150cc OHV single and we called it the Terrier which was the most apt name we could think of beginning with 'T'. It first appeared at the London Show in November 1953, and it looked like a real Triumph. It sported a small version of the nacelle headlamp, telescopic forks, familiar tank badges and the famous Speed Twin amaranth red finish. It was a simple pushrod design 57 x 58.5mm –

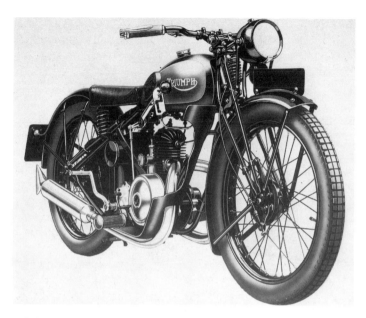

Villiers-engined lightweight, 1933, built to take advantage of a 15/- (75p) tax. Two capacities were available: 98cc and 147cc.

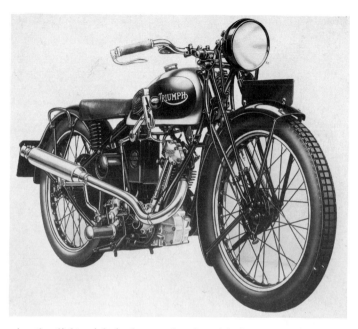

Another lightweight in the same bracket, this time a 147cc OHV fitted into the frame of the two-stroke.

149cc, compression ratio 7:1, power output 8.3bhp at 6,500rpm. It had a four-speed unit gearbox, electrics by alternator with coil ignition and plunger rear suspension.

Where you have a range of big powerful bikes, it is always a good ploy to produce a nice lightweight as well, one that has a family likeness to its big brothers. Someone taking up motorcycling for the first time starts on the little

one and when he has acquired some experience, he will want something with more performance and tends to turn to the bigger models, thus you keep him in the family as it were. He might even stay with you for the rest of his motorcycling days; some owners do become firmly attached to one manufacturer – that is how the one-make clubs start.

Turner's entry into the lightweight field was the handsome little 150cc OHV Terrier which, as can be seen here, bore a striking family resemblance to its Speed Twin big brother.

The Gaffers' Gallop

To launch the Terrier, a scheme was hatched whereby three of these models were to be ridden from Land's End to John o' Groat's under official observation plus some extra miles to bring the total to 1,000. A close check would be kept on average speed and petrol consumption and the aim was to do 30mph and 100mpg (50kph and 35km per litre). So far so good, but the clever part concerned the riders. No works trials riders were to figure, or even works testers. The riders were Edward Turner himself, Works Director Bob Fearon and Service Manager Alex Masters – who suggested this I am not sure, but it could only have been the Managing Director himself. Anyway, everything went off exactly to schedule and the target figures were handsomely beaten with 36.68mph and 108.6mpg (59kph and 38.8km per litre). This run which has been described in detail elsewhere was called 'The Gaffers' Gallop' by *Motor Cycling* magazine and proved that manufacturers do ride their own products, contrary to popular opinion! Incidentally the price of the Terrier when launched was £98 plus purchase tax in the UK, making a total of £125.4s.6d.

The Cub Arrives

A year later, in 1954, the Terrier acquired a bigger brother, the 200cc 'Tiger Cub'. It was basically the same machine, but the engine dimensions were enlarged to 63 x 64mm, bringing it up to 199cc. Compression ratio was the

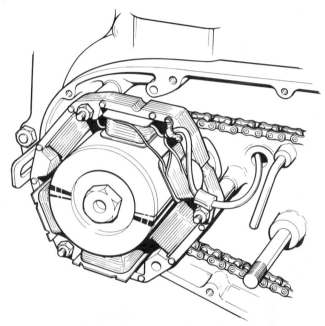

Pioneered by Triumph in 1953 this AC Lighting-Ignition unit was mounted directly on the crankshaft and replaced the separate magneto and dynamo with their attendant power-consuming chain drives. Similar alternators are now found on most cars.

same – 7:1 – and the power went up to 10bhp at 6,000rpm. So popular did the Cub become that the Terrier was deemed redundant and was dropped from the range for 1957. This was not before Jim Alves, our Number One

The Tiger Cub was an uprated version of the Terrier with a 200cc engine. It eventually replaced the Terrier.

Bob Fearon

Bob Fearon, Works Director, came to Meriden from BSA Small Heath in 1950 when Alf Camwell retired. A very likeable character with a keen sense of humour, Bob settled in well at Meriden and soon became one of the 'family'. He had not ridden a motorcycle for some time when the 'Gaffers Gallop' was proposed, but performed well and confessed afterwards to having 'enjoyed every minute'.

trials star had built himself a Terrier to ride in trials. He liked it a lot too, it was that much easier to handle than the 350 and 500 twins that he had been riding. This was where the trend to real lightweight trials bikes started. When the Cub came along, Jim transferred to it at once, as the more powerful engine was a decided asset.

From then on, the works team all rode Cubs for trials and very successful they were too. For example, in the 1959 Scottish Six Days Trial, toughest of them all, Tiger Cubs finished first, fourth and seventh, winning the Premier Award (Best Solo), the Manufacturers Team Award and the 200cc Class Award – a clean sweep! The winning rider was Roy Peplow and his team mates were Ray Sayer and Arthur Ratcliffe.

Probably the most astonishing performance with a Cub was by Bill Martin, Triumph dealer in California who, in 1959, set a new American Motorcycle Association (AMA) two-way record for 200cc machines of 139.82mph (225kph) over the measured mile. A one-way speed of 149.31mph (240.28kph) was recorded!

The Cub continued successfully for many years and was subject to steady development over that time. Sports Cubs, Trials Cubs, Competition Cubs were produced plus many others; the T20 designation grew to T20C, T20S, T20T, T20S/L, T20S/S, T20S/H, TR20, etc, etc. The French Army used Cubs extensively. It was a very good little bike which continued in production until 1968.

I have covered quite a few miles on Cubs and found them very satisfying. They handled and cornered well and

The Tiger Cub developed into a formidable competition model which claimed several important wins including, amongst others, the Scottish Six Days Trial. This is the 1961 T20S/L.

off-road they were superb, as one might expect from their competition record.

As an interesting footnote to the Cub engine design, it was perpetuated to some extent in the 250cc BSA C15 which was announced in 1958. An alloy head sat on an iron barrel and the valve gear mirrored Cub practice with tappets side by side running directly in the crankcase. Details internally were very much Cub, but one variation was the gear-driven oil pump. The series continued with other successful models like the 250cc SS80 sports, the 350cc B40 and the 440cc Victor.

Johnny Allen's 193mph (310kph) on (or in) a 650cc Triumph-engined Cigar caused a sensation. The machine was flown to England for the Earls Court Show, but employees at Meriden had the first view.

Salt Flats Sensation

The year 1955 was a noteworthy year for Triumph and demonstrated once again that we had, at this time, an uncanny way of making the headlines. It all happened in America, which was not unusual. A young man from Texas, by name Johnny Allen, driving a 14ft-long streamlined shell powered by a cast-iron 650cc Triumph engine achieved a two-way speed of 193mph (310kph) on the Bonneville Salt Flats. The streamliner, a new concept in record breakers had been designed by 'Stormy' Mangham, a forty-nine year old American Airlines pilot. The engine was basically a standard Thunderbird unit which had been built by the skilful hands of Jack Wilson, a Triumph dealer from Dallas with many years' experience in making Triumph engines go rather quicker than expected.

The following year, the German NSU company sent a powerful team to Bonneville with a supercharged 500cc twin-cylinder racer and proceeded to up the record to 211.40mph (340.20kph) and left for home amid a great blaze of publicity. A few days later, when the Germans were safely home, the Allen équipe which was backed by Bill Johnson, Pasadena distributor, wheeled out their streamliner again and proceeded to take the record back at 214mph (344kph). I do not think the Germans could have been very happy about this. The Fédération Internationale Motocycliste (FIM) refused to recognize this record due to some technicality concerning the absence of an official FIM time-keeper. No one doubted the authenticity of Allen's speed and as the Americans had hardly even heard

A presentation to Johnny Allen made by Mr Robert B Parke, First Secretary at the US Embassy. Alongside Allen is Jack Wilson who prepared the machine. Edward Turner, left in the foreground, Ivor Davies in the background.

of the FIM, they were not really bothered. However, it did lead to a lot of animosity between our factory and the governing body which dragged on for a long time.

Johnny Allen, when his streamliner days were over, moved into real estate, with equal success I believe.

We had to wait until 1962 for another streamliner to appear, this one built by Joe Dudek and driven by Bill Johnson (not our Bill Johnson) which put the record out of sight for the time being at 224.57mph (361.40kph), again with a 650cc Triumph engine. This time, the record was recognized by the FIM and we were good friends again! The argument over the Allen record produced headlines in the technical press for months afterwards, but as some shrewd commentator once said, 'There is no such thing as bad publicity'. My sentiments exactly.

One interesting result of all this activity on the Salt was that when we were casting around for a name for the new high-performance twin-carb 650, the obvious suggestion came up: 'Call it the Bonneville', and that is how the most celebrated and popular Triumph of all time got its name. To ram home the impact of these records, we brought both streamliners and their riders to England and the machines were displayed on the Triumph stand at the London Shows following.

Many years later, in 1984 or thereabouts, I discovered that Johnny Allen's machine was still in Jack Wilson's workshop and organized its purchase by the National Motorcycle Museum, Birmingham, where it proudly sits today alongside Slippery Sam and other famous racing Triumphs.

First 'Unit' Twin

Another milestone in the company's history that year was the launch of the 3TA, or model Twenty-One. This was a

The Speed Twin was redesigned. It was virtually identical to the Twenty-One apart from the 500cc engine and the amaranth red finish.

The 350cc model Twenty-One included many novel features like the very attractive rear encloser and this tool kit with the tools set in a rubber-moulded container under the seat.

350cc twin and for the first time we had a unit-construction gearbox on a twin. All the twins had unit gearboxes eventually. The name Twenty-One was double-edged; it marked our twenty-first anniversary, and in the US, where the Americans preferred inches to centimetres, the 3TA had a '21 cubic inch' engine. It was a nice-looking bike with several special features apart from the gearbox. The rear end was enclosed with stylish panelling, and under the hinged twinseat, the tool kit was mounted in rubber. Finish was shell-blue sheen with black frame. The cylinder block was iron, but finished to match the alloy head, giving the appearance of an all-alloy unit.

The 3TA engine was the first major departure from Edward Turner's 1937 format. It followed the usual pat-tern with camshafts fore and aft of the block, but the unit gearbox did alter the appearance and a much tidier engine resulted. The testing of the 3TA was very intensive, since it had so many new features, and this resulted in minimal service problems later on.

The Bonnie

The 1959 Earls Court Show in London saw a new model on the glittering Triumph stand – a model that was destined to become the most popular and prestigious ever to emerge from Meriden – the Bonneville 120, or T120 for short. It had been a last-minute decision to send the bike to London and it had come too late even to be included in the 1959 catalogue. Its development had not been a last minute rush though; it had been going on for a very long time and a full account of it will be found in John Nelson's excellent book, *Bonnie*.

The demand for more and more power never ceased, especially from the Americans and as they were by far our biggest customers it was necessary to listen very carefully to their wishes. Extracting more horsepower from an engine was a well-known science at Meriden, the experimental department had been doing it officially and unofficially for many years. After the Grand Prix, the Tiger 100 had been dealt with very successfully by making available a racing kit of go-fast parts. This experience had now been applied in the development of similar components for the T110, purely experimentally, anticipating that one day they might be incorporated in a new high-performance 650. That day came in August 1958, when after prolonged testing, the new twin-carb 650 – which the experimental department had been working on for a long time, was approved for production by the Managing Director.

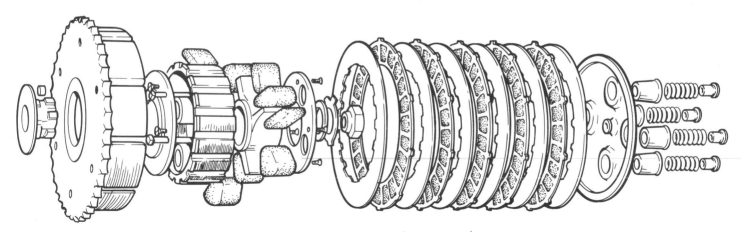

The Triumph clutch incorporated a shock absorber which comprised rubber inserts operating on both drive and rebound, resulting in a very smooth operation.

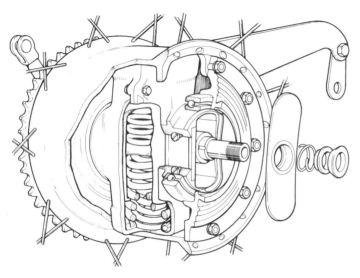

The Triumph-patented rear Spring Wheel, another very unique Triumph feature. This self-contained rear suspension system replaced the standard rigid wheel and was located in the frame in the normal manner.

The name 'Bonneville' was of course given to honour the exploits of Johnny Allen on the Salt Flats at Bonneville, Utah and this name was welcomed by the Americans, as might be expected. It was reported that the prototype weighed 404lb (183kg) and had recorded 128mph (206kph) on the electronic timing strip at the Motor Industry Research Association (MIRA), ridden by Percy Tait. Once

the Bonneville was in the hands of the customers it soon began to make a name for itself, especially in production racing where one of the highlights was Malcolm Uphill's victory in the 1969 Production TT in the Isle of Man. His race average was 99.99mph (160kph) with a record lap of 22min 33.2sec, an average speed of 100.37mph (161.5kph), the first ever lap at over 100mph (160kph) by a production motorcycle. Other Bonnevilles finished third, fifth and sixth. This same year also saw Uphill, partnered by Percy Tait, win the Thruxton 500 Mile Race. The FIM *Coupe d'Endurance* went to Triumph that year as well.

The race winners were a specially developed version of the Bonneville, known as the 'Thruxton' named after the race circuit in Hampshire. They were a very limited edition, just sufficient to satisfy the homologation rules for production racing. Work on the chassis provided better handling and the engine finally developed around 54bhp at 6,500rpm. The Thruxton was not only a consistent winner, but was also exceptionally fast. In 1969, Rodney Gould, who finished second to Malcolm Uphill, clocked 140mph (225kph) at the Highlander, a speed only exceeded by Agostini on this three-cylinder unsilenced Grand Prix model.

Tina and Others

The British motorcycle industry never got to grips properly with the scooter. When Vespa and Lambretta were first imported into the UK, they were regarded with some

The year 1959 saw the launch of what proved to be the most successful Triumph model of all time – the Bonneville. This was the first one but the nacelle was soon dropped in favour of the old-style headlamp arrangement which could be quickly removed for competition use.

amusement in those manufacturing circles busy with the production of real motorcycles. It is probably true to say that the British industry was right out of its depth in any other form of two-wheeled vehicle than the 'real' motor-

cycle. Nothing we ever produced could compete with the NSU Quickly or the Honda 50 or even the Velosolex. We did dabble in this field many times, but with a conspicuous lack of success. The BSA Dandy nearly made it, the BSA Besa, a very ambitious design of a big scooter expired before it got into production. There were quite a lot of

Triumph, like other British manufacturers was late into the scooter market and not much came of it. The Triumph Tigress was a typically curvaceous Turner creation. It had a choice of engines, 175 two-stroke or 250 OHV twin.

The Tigress engine layout. It was a neat little vertical OHV twin which provided a more than adequate performance.

autocycles, the New Hudson (by BSA) and the Norman for example, but these did not last long. The problem as I see it, was that there was no faith in the market, consequently quantities planned were too small, and to sell at the right price (dictated by the competition) specifications had to be skimped and quality sacrificed. In addition to this, in the case of big scooters we were far too late. Vespa and Lambretta created a market for themselves; their products were first class, and the market eventually faded before we could even get a foothold in it.

The BSA Group announced a scooter in October 1958. To be more specific, there were two scooters and two versions of each so there were really four scooters although they were basically the same. One was fitted with a 175cc Bantam based two-stroke and the other had a 250cc twin-cylinder engine. Each was available as a Triumph Tigress or a BSA Sunbeam. All had the same chassis details and the same transmission, but colours and badges were different. The four-speed gearbox was Tiger Cub and an electric starter was available on the twin at extra cost. The shape was very 'Turner-esque' with beautifully moulded curves to the panelling – altogether they looked very stylish and attractive. Unfortunately, this venture into the scooter world was not a success. Whether they were too sophisticated and therefore too expensive, or whether scooters were going out of fashion it is difficult to say now, but the Tigress and Sunbeam continued until 1965 when they were quietly dropped.

In 1962 another scooter came off the Turner drawing board. This was the Tina and a very ingenious little

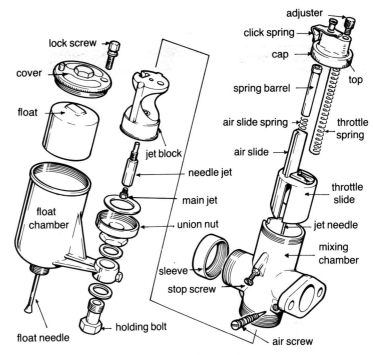

The Amal carburettor fitted to most Triumph models. Simple to maintain and tune, it provided excellent performance with maximum fuel economy.

machine it was too. You may recall that in his letter to Bill Johnson quoted earlier (*see* pages 69–70) Turner makes several references to scooters, which obviously interested him. He says there that the scooter could have a future if

The Tina scooter came later and was unique in that it had automatic transmission by belt on expanding pulleys.

(I quote), 'it is sufficiently light in construction to be parked in the household, or at any rate does not require a garage. It should be infallibly reliable in the hands of a non-technical owner; start really easily and be simple to control; but I cannot help feeling that by the time one has achieved all this, one has arrived at a vehicle that costs almost as much as a motorcycle.' Maybe the Tigress fell into the latter category, but the Tina would appear to be aimed at all the other requirements he lists. It was certainly light. With its automatic transmission it was very easy to control. It sometimes started readily, but initially it was certainly not 'infallibly reliable'. This was the problem that Bert Hopwood walked into when he rejoined Triumph. Hopwood says in his book that, 'The Tina scooter . . . was soon to cause me such anxiety and despair that, at one particular stage I seriously contemplated making a run for it and buying a small business.'

It appears that there had been very little prototype road testing, most of the proving being concerned with the automatic transmission which comprised a V belt drive across expanding pulleys. This testing was done on a workshop rig. Hopwood 'played hell' with Turner and ordered three prototypes to be built. Things then began to move and much later Turner expressed his gratitude to Hopwood, which the latter was able to appreciate rather more than most. Unfortunately, before all this extra work could be completed, the official launch date had been decided and invitations sent out inviting dealers to a luncheon party at Meriden. I well remember that event although at the time I was not aware that the Tina was in such an undeveloped state. We had an enormous marquee erected on the lawn in front of the factory and the caterers, from London, did a fabulous job in providing a piping hot three-course lunch for about 300 dealers. They cleared up and had disappeared by about 3.30pm.

A further complication concerned with this affair was that Edward Turner disappeared to America just before and left Bert Hopwood to sell the Tina scooter to the dealers. He managed it very competently too, knowing that the product was 'brilliant in conception . . . but left much to be desired in basic engineering', a fact which he did not stress to the dealers on that occasion! The work necessary to convert the Tina into a satisfactory little vehicle involved the redesign of many major items in the specification, but the design team then resident at Meriden managed it. However, by the time it was done, the volume scooter market had disappeared. Mention must be made of John Nelson, Service Manager and the late Stan Truslove, Service Engineer, on whom the brunt of the complaints from outside fell and whose efforts and ability preserved to a remarkable extent the good name of the company.

In 1965, the Tina underwent a number of fairly minor modifications and it was renamed the T10. One unusual item was moving the front brake lever to the left handlebar. This was logical as the right hand then controlled the throttle, the left had the front brake and the rear brake was foot-operated. Logical, but odd to a motorcyclist. It was now finished in flamboyant red. Press road tests spoke of 40mph (64kph) cruising, the automatic transmission working well and fuel consumption of 100mpg (36km per litre).

Maybe it was a good little bike at last – but why not right from the start?

13

Company Upheavals

Triumph Sold to BSA

The year 1951 was a notable one in Triumph history not only for the setting up of the Triumph Corporation in Baltimore (*see* Chapter 9), but also because, on 15 March to be precise, the ownership of Triumph Engineering Co Ltd passed to the Birmingham Small Arms Co Ltd (BSA for short). This has already been referred to in the piece on Jack Sangster (*see* page 41). At a meeting of the senior management at Meriden, Mr Sangster explained that when he sold Ariel to BSA in 1939, he agreed that if he ever wanted to dispose of Triumph, BSA would have first refusal. This time had now come because he was afraid that if anything happened to him, death duties would cripple the company. A price was agreed, £2,448,000 – of which Sangster claimed ninety per cent and Turner ten per cent – percentages based on their respective shareholdings. We all had a good laugh later at a tabloid press story of Sangster walking into the bank with his paying-in book and calmly handing over a cheque for £2½m to be paid into his account!

The senior management was rather alarmed at this news and there was some apprehension as to what might happen in the future. However, we need not have worried; Edward Turner was still very much in charge at Meriden and he would not have tolerated any interference from our friends and rivals up the road in Small Heath, Birmingham. In fact, nothing changed, rivalry between the two companies continued as before, which was a very healthy thing and good for both. It was a friendly relationship and help with problems was never refused, from whichever direction they came. Our respective trials riders always aimed to put it across their opposite numbers, and at Show times we always did our utmost to upstage each other with even bigger, better and brighter displays.

Boardroom Upheaval

In 1956 Sir Bernard Docker was removed as Chairman of the BSA Group and his place taken by Jack Sangster. Sir

Bernard did not give up without a struggle, but a motion he tabled to the effect that he had been dismissed without proper reference to the shareholders was defeated by 365 votes to 118. A further motion to remove Jack Sangster was also defeated, this time by 303 to 109 votes.

When the dust had settled, BSA got back to business and the BSA Automotive Division was formed with Edward Turner as Chief Executive. The Division comprised the three motorcycle companies, Ariel, BSA and Triumph, the Daimler Co Ltd, car, bus and military vehicle maker and Carbodies Ltd of Coventry, producer of the famous London taxicab.

This development affected me at the time because Turner appointed me advertising manager of the Division. My appointment was not received with any great enthusiasm at Ariel or BSA, who were used to looking after their own publicity matters and did not relish any outsider, particularly one from Triumph, telling them what to do. I certainly had no intention of doing that and by only helping when asked, we eventually got on well together and I enjoyed the change of scene.

Daimler was a different story. They welcomed me from the start and I thoroughly enjoyed producing literature for very expensive motorcars, buses and the fabulous Daimler armoured Scout Car which could motor forward or back with equal facility – very useful when suddenly faced with a nasty enemy ambush. I also enjoyed driving the expensive motorcars, which was necessary in order to write about them convincingly. They were quite a change after my own little 10hp Ford!

Turner was in his element at Daimler. It had not been profitable for years and he set about it with great enthusiasm. Cars on loan to friends of the company, titled or otherwise, were hastily withdrawn. Other non-profit making activities were scrapped and he then looked at the model range which was somewhat long in the tooth.

It was a case of 'back to the drawing board' and he soon produced two very impressive V8 engines in 2½- and 4½-litre capacities. The valve gear geometry of these engines was popularly reputed to be based on the 650 Triumph. Turner's outline specifications were turned into two superb engines by the talented Daimler engineers. The smaller engine went into a two-seat sports car called the SP250 which had a fibreglass body. The bigger engine

The Daimler SP250 Sports Car designed by Edward Turner in 1959. It had a superb 2½-litre V-eight engine and a glassfibre body shell.

went into one of the large Daimler saloons and was named the Majestic Major. Driving either of these engines was quite an experience. They were virtually inaudible and the power came in with turbine-like smoothness, whilst acceleration was breathtaking.

In 1957 the Triumph Engineering Co Ltd celebrated its twenty-first birthday with a grand dinner at the Hotel Leofric in Coventry. Edward Turner says a few words – Jack Sangster is on Turner's left. It must have been a great occasion for these two, for they had created this very successful company.

You are probably asking yourself by this time, 'Why are we reading all this about Daimler in a Triumph book?' We will get back to Triumph in a minute but Turner's activities up the road at Daimler did affect Triumph because we did not see so much of him. This resulted in a more peaceful life for everyone at Meriden, although Turner still managed to cope with both factories and remained very much in charge.

A Birthday

The year 1957 marked the twenty-first anniversary of the Triumph Engineering Co Ltd and this was celebrated by a dinner at the Leofric Hotel in Coventry, attended by a large contingent of employees and all the major suppliers, plus (of course) the press. The hotel is situated just a short distance from where the old Priory Street works were located before it was destroyed, so it was an appropriate venue. Charles Parker presented Edward Turner with a very nice mantel clock. Speeches were made by Jack Sangster, Turner and Parker and one or two others I seem to recall, and a very happy evening resulted.

Changes at the Top

In 1960, Eric Turner (no relation to Edward) joined the BSA Board as Chief Executive and Deputy Chairman. He was a forty-two year old qualified accountant, previously Chairman of Blackburn and General Aircraft. This appointment was obviously made with a view to the fact that Jack Sangster would be retiring in 1961 at the age of sixty-five. One wonders why these appointments always seemed to go to 'outsiders' with no knowledge of the company or its products. With hindsight, and in view of what happened subsequently, one wonders even more.

In June 1961, Jack Sangster did retire, although still retaining a directorship. He handed over the BSA Group to Eric Turner with a record profit that year of £3,418,000. This was also the centenary year of BSA, and it was fitting that it should reach it in a healthy financial position. The same year was also notable for the return of Bert Hopwood to Triumph after his fourteen-year stint away. He was at Norton from April 1947 to May 1949 when he joined BSA. He remained there until April 1955 when he accepted an offer from Associated Motorcycles Ltd which brought Norton under his control again. In his book *Whatever Happened to the British Motorcycle Industry?*, Hopwood describes how he was approached by Edward Turner, very persistently, to come back to Meriden as Turner's health was not good and he anticipated an early retirement. He goes on to say:

I realized that he [Turner] was just as self-opinionated as he had ever been, but this failing, if failing it be, never really mattered to anyone with a sense of humour. I must say that I never believed it possible that I should experience such persistent approaches with the culminating final revealing statement that he could not afford to make a mistake in this important matter and had come to the conclusion that I was the only man with the experience and background to support him during the transition and carry on with the job after his retirement. This was quite a new experience for me, for compliments of any description from this source were a rarity to be cherished. I do admit that I was so pleasantly surprised that this seemed to be the decisive factor and I agreed to join the Triumph Board in May 1961, as Director and General Manager.

Needless to say, everyone at Meriden was pleased to see Bert Hopwood again, it was quite like old times. Edward Turner was still Chief Executive of the BSA Automotive Division but there had been some changes. Daimler had been sold to Jaguar, much I believe to Turner's dismay. His 2½-litre V8 engine was slotted into the Mark II Jaguar saloon and rumour has it that it became one of the best cars in the Jaguar range – the lighter V8 unit making a considerable difference to the general feel and handling of the car.

Turner Goes to Japan

Competition from Japan in the late fifties and early sixties was hotting up, and Edward Turner paid a visit to that country in 1960 to see what was happening. I will pick out the salient points from his report.

Turner said that as a result of the tremendous growth of the Japanese industry, it was decided that he should go to Japan, examine their organizations, visit their factories,

*In 1960 Edward Turner reconnoitred the Japanese
motorcycle industry and did not like what he saw! Here,
he is seen with Mr Honda himself.*

observe manufacturing methods and, if possible, discuss Japanese plans for exporting so that we could formulate counter measures to preserve our own share of world motorcycle markets.

He had previously examined certain Yamaha, Honda and Suzuki products and formed a very high opinion of their designs, finish and manufacturing accuracy, 'but no im-

pression I had gained of the obvious upsurge of this important industry bore any relation to the shocks I received on closer examination of this situation on their home ground'. He continued:

Japan has 90 million highly intelligent, very energetic purposeful people, all geared to an economic machine with the avowed object of becoming great again, this time in the world of business and industry, and nothing, apparently, is going to stop them. Today, with Japanese-manufactured goods of all types, the accent is on quality. They are fully aware of the reputation they have to live down. Japan today is the largest manufacturer of motorcycles in the world, all of excellent quality . . . one company . . . produces more motorcycles than the whole British industry together . . . they are producing well over half a million motorcycles a year (against 140,000 British).

The speed with which Japanese motorcycle companies can produce new designs and properly tested and developed models is startling . . . Honda alone has an establishment of 400 technicians engaged in studying new manufacturing techniques, new designs, new developments and new approaches. Unlike our own country there is an enormous pool of well trained brains to be had at nominal cost. Wages of course, by our standards are very low . . . but it should be borne in mind that . . . the workpeople live in company-owned houses and pay less than a dollar a month rent, and buy food at cost. Also . . . when an industrial enterprise employs them, it keeps them on the payroll through good times and bad.

Yamaha Shopfloor scene not dissimilar from Triumph but with more movement, particularly of components . . . machine tool equipment was first class and new.

Suzuki Their principals had visited Triumph . . . and were willing to discuss any aspect of their business with me. Their factory was even more mechanized than Yamaha and very self-contained making its own castings, forgings, presswork etc.

Honda Mr Honda expressed great respect for the British industry and felt that though some of our products were old-fashioned, he was not deceived by this and thought that the 350/500cc range of Triumph was equal in comparison with anything made in Japan. The Honda factory had everything that one could desire as an up-to-date manufacturing conception for motorcycles.

Testing in all factories was done on rollers geared to brakes which gave horsepower readings while the machine was stationary. A final run round the test track seemed to suffice to ensure roadworthy standards.

It is essential that our industry in general and the BSA Group in particular should know the facts and what we are up against in the retention of our export markets. Even our home market will be assailed. . .[!]

By and large, the menace of Japanese motorcycles to our own export markets is that they are producing extremely refined and well finished motorcycles up to 300cc at prices which reach the public at something like twenty per cent less. The machines are more comprehensive than our own in regard to equipment such as electric starting, traffic indicators etc. It should be borne in mind that the motorcycle industry has never been big business in Britain. We have never made to date, even in these relatively boom times, 1,000 units of any one product in a week consistently, whereas many factories in Japan are currently doing this in a day.

I have given considerable thought to what we might do and must confess that the answers are going to be hard to find. One of the most practical thoughts in this present situation would be to visualize opening up our own motorcycle operations in Japan . . . we might even, should we consider this, obtain technical help which is not to be despised, particularly in regard to our future tooling and development.

It is obvious that Edward Turner was very considerably shaken by what he saw in Japan. The scale of the business there was right out of sight of anything ever seen in the UK. When you are making millions of motorcycles, the quality can be high and this sells them, and for the same reason the price can be low, or certainly lower than the competition. The Japanese not only made motorcycles in vast quantities, but also created the markets worldwide that could buy them.

We never contemplated anything on this scale in our wildest dreams.

14

Turner Retires

Bert Hopwood rejoined Triumph in 1961 as Director and General Manager and I quoted him earlier describing how Edward Turner persuaded him to come back on the basis that he (Edward Turner) intended to retire and that Hopwood was the only man he knew who could take his place when this happened (flattery will get you everywhere!). Eventually, in 1964, Turner did retire, but he retained his directorship on the BSA Board.

It was about this time that Japanese competition began to make itself felt. Edward Turner's visit to Japan (*see* Chapter 13) sheds some light on the subject.

The theory which had been put about by certain senior personnel in the industry was that the Japanese only made small bikes and this was fine for us because the powerful Japanese advertising campaigns, particularly in America, were persuading a whole lot of new customers to take to two wheels. Now, the theory went, when these owners of small Japanese bikes wanted more performance, as they undoubtedly would, they would be obliged to buy British. This was probably the most fatuous theory ever advanced in the history of the British motorcycle industry, and it might have been true for a short time, but our friends from the land of the rising sun found out that the big money was in the big bikes. They probably knew this right from the start and were just testing the temperature of the water with the little bikes. Once they started to move up the capacity scale, it boded ill for us, as we were soon to find out.

Bert Hopwood, in his book, describes how, at a meeting of our sales and marketing personnel, one of the sales managers casually mentioned that he had heard that the Japanese would be announcing a 750 very soon. This caused a great stir and Harry Sturgeon (late of the aircraft and machine tool industries) who had taken over as Managing Director from Edward Turner demanded to know what we were going to do about it? Now, Bert Hopwood and Doug Hele had been working unofficially on a 750cc three-cylinder engine for some time past, and the drawings for this were produced. Sturgeon gave instructions for prototypes to be built as quickly as possible and that was how the famous Triumph Trident and BSA Rocket Three models came into being. More about this later.

Turner Retires Finally

It will be remembered that in 1964 Edward Turner retired as Chief Executive of the BSA Automotive Division, retaining his position on the BSA Board. In 1967 he retired from the BSA Board, so that ended his connection with the Group altogether. He was then sixty-six years of age and had served the industry well. He had designed products that had sold in large numbers and brought prosperity to their companies which had been teetering on the verge of bankruptcy for a long time.

He had recognized the potential market for motorcycles in the United States when there was virtually no market for motorcycles there at all, let alone British ones. Together with Bill Johnson Jnr (not to be confused with the Bill Johnson of Salt Flats fame), Denis McCormack and their employees he had created a market in the States that in a relatively short space of time absorbed the major part of Meriden's output for many years. Even that was not enough. Harry Holland, Meriden's Export Manager for many years told me:

It was never possible to ship to Johnson Motors or the Triumph Corporation quantities sufficient to fully satisfy either, notwithstanding that the export share of Meriden production was sixty per cent (leaving forty per cent for the UK.)

Other British manufacturers benefited from this situation and later, when the industry began to lag behind its

Johnson Motors Inc, California – the magnificent showrooms built by Bill Johnson to sell Triumph products.

The year 1971 should have seen this 350cc DOHC twin, the Bandit, in production. Its initial design was produced by Edward Turner. Severe financial difficulties caused the project to be abandoned.

Japanese competitors, the latter were able to move into the States and take over a ready-made chain of very experienced dealers which was greatly to their benefit. A sorry situation for the British, but that is what happened.

Turner will always be remembered for his creation of the modern vertical twin-cylinder engine which first appeared in 1937. Such was its success that other manufacturers were left wondering where their next sales were coming from. They were all obliged to produce something similar to compete with the Speed Twin (and Tiger 100), which they did, but the war intervened and these rival twins did not come on the scene until hostilities had ceased. The Japanese, much later, were forced to tread the same path, as were the Continentals. But, not content with two cylinders, the Japanese followed on with a dazzling assortment of fours in straight, V and flat formations. Then came six-cylinders, across the frame, but they were a little over the top and it was the fours that sold. These, with their electric starters and many other refinements made their European competitors look a trifle dated.

It was Edward Turner and his Speed Twin that revitalized the British industry after the war and nothing can take that credit away from him. His other and earlier masterpiece, the Ariel Square Four, was a fine motorcycle but in no way did it cause the upheaval in the industry produced by the Speed Twin. Turner's last design, a 350cc DOHC twin for the Group, he did as a freelance in 1970, after his retirement. This did not reach the market as the Group collapsed before it could do so.

He died at home on 15 August 1973.

15

Triumph Goes Racing

When Edward Turner finally retired in 1967, his position was taken by Harry Sturgeon. Sturgeon, unlike Turner, was convinced that Triumph would have to race to maintain its position in world markets and particularly in the United States. This was a complete about-face as far as Meriden was concerned. Turner considered that producing exotic racers that bore little or no relation to the showroom models apart from the name on the tank was not only a waste of money, but a waste also of the best engineering brains in the company. Norton had suffered in this way for many years. They had built superb racers that won everything going, but their standard production motorcycles were not exactly winners in the showroom.

Daytona

The annual Daytona Races were the major events in the American racing calendar and the decision was made that Triumph would 'have a go' at Daytona in 1966. The only competitive 500cc motorcycle in the Group was the Triumph Tiger 100 and a quick development programme was initiated under the guidance of Doug Hele. Doug's experience in this field was extensive, having been at Norton during their racing heyday.

The Triumph 500cc engine was a durable piece of engineering in everyday use, but Daytona was a rather different proposition. Here it would be driven flat out for 200 miles (320km) at speeds around the 120/130 (190/210) mark. This was asking a lot of a relatively simple twin-cylinder pushrod engine not designed as a racer.

A programme of modifications was therefore planned to increase the performance of the engine. Valve angles were changed, inlet valves enlarged, 9.75 'pent roof' pistons fitted and extensive lightening and polishing was carried out to other components. An oil cooler was mounted forward of the engine.

Good handling was vital and modifications to the frame

In 1966 Triumph won the prestigious Daytona Race with this remarkable Tiger 100 which had seen much high pressure development in the preceding months. The rider was the American Buddy Elmore.

The Daytona engine had two Amal carburettors with remote rubber-suspended racing float bowls. An oil cooler was mounted forward of the engine and the exhaust camshaft drove the Lucas racing contact breaker unit.

included a new headlug with additional bracing and a stiffened rear swinging arm. Standard forks, brakes and wheels were used, but the latter had alloy rims. Four machines were prepared and were shipped to the States early in March 1966. Riders were supplied by the two American distributors, Johnson Motors Inc and Triumph Corporation, two from each. The race is fully described in John Nelson's book *Triumph Tiger 100/Daytona*, so that all I need mention here is that the winner was Buddy Elmore, on one of our works prepared Tigers, who came from behind to take the lead on lap 20 and held it to the end.

With a year to incorporate the lessons learned in 1966, the 1967 Tiger 100 racers, six of them this time, repeated their winning performance with Gary Nixon in Number One spot, hotly chased by Buddy Elmore. All six machines finished in the first fifteen places, out of ninety-seven starters, thus did the T100/Daytona get its name! It is interesting to note that many of the race-winning features of the 1967 racers were incorporated in the standard production T100 by 1969. If therefore you should ask that time-honoured queston: 'Does racing improve the breed?', I can honestly answer, 'Yes' in the case of the Tiger 100 of this period.

Triumph has always had a curious 'love-hate' relationship with racing, at least whilst Edward Turner was in charge. To be fair he did say that if racing for production motorcycles was ever organized, then Triumph would support it. After he had retired, production racing was organized and Triumph did support it, but the decision was not made by Turner obviously. Bert Hopwood was the man who launched Triumph into an incredibly successful racing session in the seventies with the three-cylinder that he and Doug Hele had designed, which by then incorporated features from the race-winning Tiger 100s.

The Racing 'Threes'

Triumph racing successes really started when Percy Tait, that legendary figure at Meriden, was entered for the Hutchinson 100 in 1969 on a factory-prepared three. He finished sixth, but the ride was intended to check handling rather than to win the race. This proved satisfactory and work started on the engine. This involved fitting certain race-proven components from the successful 500, the two engines being basically similar. An output of 78bhp resulted, but highlighted certain ignition problems. These were suitably dealt with.

At this time, interest was growing in Formula 750 or Daytona type racing, where basically standard specifications were required, but quite extensive modifications were permitted. The value of this to a manufacturer was obvious. He could test new solutions to problems and build up a store of knowledge which could later find its way into production. Production racing, on the other hand, banned all development of this kind. Another factor which entered the scene at this time was a change in the rules by the Americans who had hitherto limited OHV engines to 500cc and side-valves to 750cc. 750cc was now the limit for all types and this encouraged the factory to enter the threes

*Ray Pickrell, one of the more successful Trident pilots.
In 1972 he won both the Production TT
and the Formula 750 event in the Isle of Man.*

at Daytona in 1970. The 500s had won in 1966 and 1967, but a more ambitious attack was planned for the threes. Six machines would go, but much new design work was put in hand before the bikes left for the States. A five-speed gearbox by Rod Quaife and a completely new frame by Rob North were two vitally important items. Fairings based on wind-tunnel research made a big contribution to a one-way speed of 164mph (264kph).

At Daytona the threes caused a great sensation by recording the three fastest times in the qualifying tests. Gene Romero clocking 157.34mph (253.20kph) with 165.44mph (266.24kph) through a speed trap on the front straight. Overheating caused problems in the race due to the fairings directing hot air on to the carburettors, but Romero and Castro finished second and third behind Dick Mann on a Honda 4, after Nixon, on one of the threes, had led for much of the race as he did again in 1967. These problems were soon fixed and in the Isle of Man, Malcolm Uphill won the Production TT and Paul Smart and Tom Dickie won the *Bol d'Or* 24-hour race in France against strong works opposition, at an average speed of 76.51mph (123.12kph) for 1,828 miles (2,494.2km) – twenty-four laps better than the record.

Then followed two years of almost unbroken success for the Tridents. Virtually every major Production and Formula 750 race was won, race records and lap records went by the board. John Cooper caused a major sensation by defeating Giacomo Agostini, the reigning World Champion, not once but twice! Agostini's MV three-cylinder was the most advanced Grand Prix model of its day and to finish second to a roadster-based racer was quite incredible – but Cooper's fantastic riding ability certainly played a part!

The other even more astonishing performance was winning the Production TT five years running, 1971–1975, with the same machine, the celebrated Slippery Sam which has now been retired honourably to the National Motorcycle Museum.

In the seventies the three-cylinder Triumph Trident reigned supreme in Production and Formula 750 racing, winning in the Isle of Man and on most other circuits of the time.

Tony Jefferies, another ace performer, on his way here to winning the 1973 Production TT. He is riding 'Slippery Sam', the famous Trident which won the Production TT in the Isle of Man for five consecutive years – 1971 to 1975.

245mph at Bonneville

Johnny Allen, Jess Thomas and Bill Johnson were three daring young men who had motored their Triumph-engined streamliners across the Salt Flats at well in excess of 200mph (320kph), Bill Johnson finally clocking 224.57mph (361.40kph) under FIM supervision and gaining the official world record title. This was in 1962.

The FIM engine capacity limit at that time was 1,000cc and the Americans had never paid much attention to this or to the FIM for that matter. Harley Davidson and Indian had always sold motorcycles with engines well over 1,000cc so that record breaking with big engines had always been the norm in the US.

The owners of a big Triumph dealership in Detroit, Michigan, Bob Leppan and Joe Brudflodt, decided to build a double-engined streamliner with two Tiger 110 non-unit engines, 1,298cc. These were set up in tandem, driving through a standard Triumph gearbox and installed in a glassfibre streamlined shell. This was 17ft 9in (5.4m) in length from nose to tail, 3ft (914mm) high and with 3in (76mm) ground clearance.

In August 1966, with this projectile, Leppan recorded a two-way average of 245.6mph (395.2kph) with the engines running on straight alcohol. The machine was named Gyronaut X-1, as at one time it was intended to use a gyroscope to aid stability, although this was never done. In 1970 two Trident three-cylinder engines had been installed in Gyronaut with the intention of attacking the record by Cal Rayborn with a Harley Davidson of 265.5mph (427kph). Unfortunately the front suspension of Gyronaut collapsed at 270mph (434kph) and Leppan was very seriously injured. Happily he made a good recovery, but Gyronaut has not been seen again and the days of Triumph-engined 'cigars' seem to be over.

They were exciting times and although we at the factory were not directly involved, both Johnny Allen and Bill Johnson, as I said earlier, came over to England with their machines which were displayed at the factory for the workforce to see. Luckily also, there happened to be Earls Court Shows both years, so that we were able to show off the streamliners to the crowds in London where they attracted an enormous amount of attention. We stood them on a long low plinth at the exhibition, the top of which, under the machine, was covered with an inch of salt – not genuine Salt Flats salt, but no matter, it looked just the same!

An extra bonus in Johnny Allen's case occurred when we took the machine to a local RAF airfield where the CO kindly permitted Johnny to motor up and down the runway for the benefit of the press, who obtained some good photographs.

One of the problems with a streamliner of this type is that it has nothing to keep it upright when stationary: the support crew should be on hand to catch it. We did not know this, so that at the end of the runway the shell, with Allen in it, rolled gently on its side as it stopped. Fortunately no damage was done.

16

Managing Directors
Come and Go

Edward Turner was replaced by Harry Sturgeon in 1967. Sturgeon was a very likeable, energetic salesman who had held a high executive position in the aircraft industry, but more recently had been Managing Director of the Churchill Grinding Machine Company, a BSA subsidiary. Sadly, his term of office was a short one and he died three years later from a brain tumour. His place was taken by another 'outside' candidate, Lionel Jofeh. The latter initiated the very expensive Umberslade Hall Group Engineering Centre which eventually housed most of the engineers and designers from the main factories. This cost a lot of money and produced very little apart from a new common frame for the Triumph and BSA twins which was so high off the ground that you had to be a giant to manage it. Despite all the criticism at the time, it went into production and had to be corrected later by Bert Hopwood at considerable expense.

Another disaster of the Jofeh era was the Ariel 3 – a moped with two wheels at the rear which was hinged centrally so that it could be leaned into corners, like a two-wheeler, with the rear wheels remaining squarely on the ground. The engine was a 50cc Anker two-stroke of Dutch origin. This was mounted above the rear axle and drove through an automatic clutch. Only the left wheel was driven or braked, and it was connected to the countershaft by chain. All wheels were interchangeable. The front frame comprised pressings and supported a trailing link fork with rubber suspension. The front brake matched the rear and Dunlop 2 x 12in tyres were fitted to the pressed-steel wheels. The hood over the rear wheels was hinged for access to the engine and could carry a shopping basket. Very ingenious, but once in production so many problems arose that only a handful were sold, despite the predictions of the market researchers. Those that did reach the public were unreliable and unstable. A figure of £2M has been quoted as the loss made on the Ariel 3 project.

Jofeh left, to be replaced by Brian Eustace, a forty-nine year old ex-GKN executive. It was strange that the

Board, or perhaps the Chairman Eric Turner, appeared to think that there was no one already in the organization who could fill this position and always went outside for a Managing Director. Charles Parker or Bert Hopwood could have done the job more than adequately in my opinion. They might even have done it better as joint Managing Directors. Not only were Board members brought in from outside either: I well remember the influx of young executives who joined us at high salaries and with nice motor cars thrown in. They knew absolutely nothing about motorcycles, but this did not worry them, motorcycles were just products, 'consumer durables' they called them! We were deluged with charts and graphs and critical path analysis programmes when all we needed, and desperately, was a range of really good motorcycles to sell.

The outcome of the constant management changes and some of the doubtful products of the period resulted in a loss of £8.5M being incurred by the Group in 1971. I have always felt that, unlike Jack Sangster and Edward Turner, the managements we had at this time were not committed to, or really interested in, motorcycles or motorcycling and this showed in the results. Motorcycles to them were rather downmarket products and they would have preferred something with a little more class.

Profits and Losses

In 1956 when Jack Sangster became Chairman, profits before tax were £1,604,000. By 1960, when he handed

Harry Sturgeon, the dynamic Managing Director who might have changed for the better the way the Group was operating, but died before this could come to fruition.

over to Eric Turner, an all-time record profit of £3,418,000 went with the hand-over. Profits earned by Triumph alone have never been officially disclosed, but it has appeared in print that between 1950 and 1969 the average annual profit was £644,000. This was a superb record for a small company and reflected great credit on all those at Meriden during this period.

As I said earlier, Jofeh was replaced by Brian Eustace and by 1971 Eric Turner had gone. Lord Shawcross, who

In an attempt to economize, the Meriden works were closed, the BSA marque was abandoned and Triumph production of the Trident was moved to the BSA works at Small Heath. This was a corner of the assembly track, April 1974.

had been a non-executive director, was asked to take over as Chairman which I believe he did rather unwillingly. Despite the efforts of the newly re-constituted board of directors, a loss of £3,300,000 was recorded at the end of July 1972. It was obvious that things could not go on much longer and discussions were started with the Department of Trade and Industry. As this book is primarily about the Edward Turner era, I do not propose to go into too much

The Triumph 750cc 'Saint' ('stops anything in no time') a famous police motorcycle used in vast numbers by London's Metropolitan Police and many other forces worldwide.

detail here as to what happened afterwards as that story has been told in full elsewhere.

A new company, Norton-Villiers-Triumph was formed which was basically an amalgam of the two major manufacturing groups, Norton and BSA, and this came into being in July 1973. Edward Turner, who had been a sick man for some time prior to this, died on 15 August 1973. This was sad, but at least he did not live to see the total destruction of the company he had created as well as his factory at Meriden which was demolished in 1984 to make way for a housing estate.

The setting up of a two-factory industry, Norton at Wolverhampton and BSA/Triumph at Small Heath, Birmingham, meant the closure of Meriden and this was something the workforce there could not stomach. They staged a sit-in which went on for a long time. In the end, after endless argument and the production of numerous plans by both sides, a co-operative was formed at Meriden in March 1975 with a Government loan of £4.2M. The intention was to re-introduce the Bonneville, now enlarged to 750cc. By these means Triumph was saved from extinction, but not for very long.

Tridents From Birmingham

Whilst all this trauma had been going on at Meriden, production of the three-cylinder Trident, uprated to T160, had started at the Small Heath factory, BSA's headquarters in Birmingham. It was ironic to see the large posters outside the BSA works advertising the Triumph Trident! No more BSAs were to be made, a sad blow to this famous marque which had been in continuous production at Small Heath since about 1910. This great company, which had been founded in 1861 as gun makers, had produced staggering quantities of military hardware in both World Wars. It had been a prime target for the *Luftwaffe* who had bombed it successfully, but failed to put it out of action.

They got going very quickly on the Trident and the fact that all three-cylinder engines for both Triumph and BSA had been made there right from the start was a great help. Frames, forks, tanks, wheels and brakes were no problem. This new Trident had the sloping cylinders of the Rocket 3, duplex primary chain, left-foot gearchange, electric starter, 4 into 2 exhaust and disc brakes front and rear. It was a very handsome motorcycle and everyone was very optimistic that it would do something to restore the fortunes of the Group. At last, we reckoned, we had a luxury multi-cylinder motorcycle that could look the Japanese opposition squarely in the face.

Meanwhile, at Kitts Green, we were making preparations for the show at Earls Court, and were looking forward to ten days or so in London; ten days of hard work, but a refreshing change from the traumas of the past few weeks in the Midlands. The show stand had been designed, the contractors appointed, the literature printed, the staffing arrangements finalized and (hopefully) all the other thousand-and-one details connected with any exhibition had been sorted out. As we (myself and the sales staff) were about to set out for the great metropolis,

Exhibitions were always a major event in our sales year. Earls Court in the fifties attracted vast crowds, as can be seen here. Johnny Allen's record-breaker is almost submerged in the crowd.

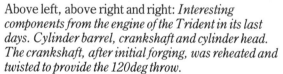

Above left, above right and right: *Interesting components from the engine of the Trident in its last days. Cylinder barrel, crankshaft and cylinder head. The crankshaft, after initial forging, was reheated and twisted to provide the 120deg throw.*

Here is a convivial scene among the Triumph distributors at the Tel Aviv Trade Fair 1966. The author (third from left) endeavours to keep out of sight.

we were informed by our Managing Director, very courteously, that our services would not be required after the end of the month (October 1975). That was a tremendous morale boost to executives about to do an intensive selling job in London in a last ditch effort to save the company!

We went to London; we did our best, and tried to forget the fact that we would be out of work at the end of the show. The bikes looked fine and the public showed a lot of interest. Despite this, we all knew that this would be the very last exhibition that we would ever set up on behalf of the BSA Group (or NVT as we were then designated).

It was the end of the British motorcycle industry as we had known it. Fortunately most of us had also known it in its great days, and nowhere had it been greater than during the fabulous Edward Turner years at Meriden.

Postscript

Triumph Again!

We have told in this book how Triumph originated, how Siegfried Bettmann established the name and ran the business for fifty years and how it was rescued from the depression of the thirties by Jack Sangster and Edward Turner. The retirement of Sangster and Turner and the gradual demise of the British motorcycle industry which followed brought Triumph to its knees again, along with BSA, Norton and other famous names.

However, a new rescuer appeared in the eighties in the form of John Bloor who, with ample finance behind him, bought the Triumph name and everything that goes with it with the firm intention of producing a completely new range of machines bearing the famous Triumph name. A brand new factory was built at Hinckley in Leicestershire, designers got busy and the factory was equipped with the latest in high-tech production equipment.

The culmination of all this prodigious effort was seen for the first time at the Cologne Motor Cycle Show in the autumn of 1990. Enthusiasts there gazed in wonder at the

The new Trident 750 has three cylinders like its forbear, but there the similarity ends! This short-stroke DOHC 12-valve triple delivers a smooth 90bhp.

space-age Triumph range which presented itself as a worthy British competitor (at last!) to the all-conquering Japanese. It was a low-key launch by Cologne standards and the Bloor organization is obviously waiting, very wisely, for the new models to be rolling off the tracks before it starts blowing any trumpets.

The engines, 3-cylinder 750/900cc and 4-cylinder 1000/1200cc are water-cooled with twin overhead camshafts and four valves per cylinder. The claimed brake horse-power figures should provide a more than adequate performance. Full fairings are specified for the Daytona and Trophy models but the Tridents are unfaired.

Hopefully, by the time this book is published, this new range should be in full production and Triumph will be on its way once more to resurrect its world-beating past.

A Six-Model Range

Using famous names from the past, the range comprised the following:

Daytona 750	3 cylinders	90bhp	Fully faired
Daytona 1000	4 cylinders	121bhp	” ”
Trophy 900	3 cylinders	100bhp	Fully faired
Trophy 1200	4 cylinders	141bhp	” ”
Trident 750	3 cylinders	90bhp	Unfaired
Trident 900	3 cylinders	100bhp	”

Appendix I

Ninety-Six of the Best

Earlier in this book I named some of the people who from pre-war days were still with Triumph in the years that followed the war. Now I would like to move on and place on record *as many names as I personally can remember* of those who were with the company after the war and stayed, in many cases, to the bitter end. For twenty years or so, this was an exciting period when Triumph was at its zenith, under dynamic leadership and with a range of first class products. The situation then deteriorated and did finally come to a *very* bitter end, the rights and wrongs of which I do not intend to go into here. After this, most of us were fortunate enough to find other gainful employment which kept us solvent until retirement.

We had a good crowd at Meriden, friendly and helpful at all times. We still meet for the occasional reunion and keep in touch in various other ways. During those years, 1946 onwards, there were not too many changes in the personnel. There were retirements of course, and some additions to the ranks from time to time to cope with the ever increasing activity. Here, I propose just to name names, that's all. To make personal comments about the people I know and with whom I worked would be much too embarrassing for us all!

No doubt there are many names missing for which I offer my apologies in advance, my excuse being that we have moved on forty years or so and these are the people I can remember – with considerable warmth in most cases.

Stan Truslove

A larger-than-life character, there was never a dull moment when Stan was around. He was a Service Engineer who knew his job from A to Z, equally adept at building sophisticated racing engines or sorting problems on the little T10 scooters to which he was assigned for a time. After the crash, he moved to Jaguar, dealing with customers worries on their motorcars. His early death in 1985 shocked his many friends in the industry.

A nicely posed picture of a motorcycle policeman in action. His Triumph is fully equipped with radio and every other modern convenience designed to deter evildoers.

It would be a very worthwhile exercise to compile a list of the whole company for the record. However, someone better equipped than me would have to do it. It would be a nice tribute to all those who should be remembered for their contribution to a very successful company.

Peter Adcock ◆ Max Ayris ◆ Frank Baker ◆ Alf Barker ◆ Reg Ballard ◆ John Barton ◆ Len Bayliss ◆ Claire Bourne ◆ Steve Bourne ◆ Peter Britton ◆ Alf Camwell ◆ Freddie Clarke ◆ Bert Coles ◆ Arthur Copson ◆ Ted Crabtree ◆ Phil Cross ◆ Merle Dawson ◆ Bill Fannon ◆ Bob Fearon ◆ Vic Fidler ◆ Jack Field ◆ Janet Fletcher ◆ 'Goldie' Goldsmith ◆ Harry Goodby ◆ Eddie Gough ◆ Charles Grandfield ◆ David Green ◆ Fred Green ◆ Steve Green ◆ Frank Griffiths ◆ Gordon Griffiths ◆ Len Hamilton ◆ Hughie Hancox ◆ Norris Harrison ◆ Sheila Hawkins ◆ Eric Headlam ◆ Doug Hele ◆ John Hickson ◆ Harry Holland ◆ Bert Hopwood ◆ Norman Hyde ◆ Don Jacquest ◆ Arthur Jakeman ◆ Brian Jones ◆ David Jones ◆ Olivia Kearns ◆ John Legge ◆ Bill Lindon ◆ John McDonnell ◆ Alan Magill ◆ Bob Manns ◆ Alec Masters ◆ 'Mat' Mathieu ◆ Les Mattocks ◆ John Nelson ◆ Ernie Nott ◆ Charles Parker ◆ Stuart Pearce ◆ Nan Plant ◆ Doreen Powell ◆ Joan Powell ◆ Malcolm Prestage ◆ Brenda Price ◆ Geoff Price ◆ Bill Robertson ◆ Ian Rush ◆ Jack Rushton ◆ Jack Sangster ◆ Alex Scobie ◆ Neale Shilton ◆ Jack Shortland ◆ Bert Smith ◆ Tyrell Smith ◆ Dick Staples ◆ Harry Summers ◆ Fred Swift ◆ Percy Tait ◆ Frank Thompson ◆ George Tilley ◆ Steve Tilley ◆ Stan

This famous photograph has not been seen for a long time. Taken at the Victory Parade on the Mall, London, on 8 June 1946, it shows the Metropolitan Police squad passing the saluting base on their Speed Twins.

A bunch of Triumph-mounted Paris policemen who helped us in the production of a film about Triumph back in 1954. The bikes are Thunderbirds, needless to say.

Neale Shilton

Neale joined Triumph exactly two weeks after me in 1946 and did a very effective sales job both in the home market and overseas. He later concentrated successfully on sales to police forces. He developed the 650cc Triumph 'Saint' model for the men in blue and claimed that the title, which he had invented, stood for 'Stops Anything In No Time'! A great enthusiast for motorcycling, he rode a bike daily, summer and winter, for the pure joy of it. He died in 1990 in Denmark, where he had lived after retirement.

Truslove ◆ Syd Tubb ◆ Edward Turner ◆ Henry Vale ◆ Jack Welton ◆ John Walford ◆ Tommy Wallace ◆ Les Warren ◆ Horace Watson ◆ Geoff Watson ◆ Fred Wickes ◆ Jack Wickes ◆ Les Williams ◆ Bill Winters ◆ Harry Woolridge ◆ Joan Wright ◆ Frank Wright

Appendix II

Useful Addresses

United Kingdom
Triumph Owners' Motor Cycle Club
Sec Mrs Margaret Mellish
4 Douglas Avenue
Harold Wood
Romford
Essex RM3 0UT
Tel: (04023) 42684

Overseas Representatives

New Zealand
Mark Steele
42 Trinidad Road
Forrest Hill
Auckland 10

Spain
Jim Everett
Bar 'El Cid'
Ye Olde English Pub
Calle Animas 16
Sitges
Barcelona

Triumph Service and Parts

Hughie Hancox
11 Burbury Close
Marston Vale Estate
Marston Lane
Bedworth
Coventry CV12 8DU
Tel: (0203) 368038

Norman Hyde
Rigby Close
Heathcote
Warwickshire CV34 6TL
Tel: (0926) 497375

LJ Williams
Common Lane Industrial Estate
Kenilworth
Warwickshire CV8 2EL
Tel: (0926) 549948

For a wide range of owners' handbooks and workshop manuals, reproduced from the original, and for a complete catalogue, write to:

JR Technical Publications
Potterdike House
Lombard Street
Newark
Nottinghamshire NG24 1XG

Index

Alfa-Romeo 40
Allen, Johnny 116–7, 143
Amal carburettor 123
American market 66–90
Andrews, William 13
Ariel, Motors (JS) Ltd 42
    Square Four 46

Baker, Frank 52
Band, C J 19
Bettmann, Annie 19
Bettmann, Siegfried 4, 12–19, 40, 41, 43
Bettmann & Company 13
Bloor, John 151
Booth Bros 14, 15
Brandish, Walter 29
Brooklands 36
Brown, Don 88
BSA 6, 126

Camwell, Alf 49
Carbodies Ltd 6, 127
Child, Alfred R 80–2
chronology (100 Years of Triumph) 1–3
Clarke, Freddie 58
Coates, Rod 88
Coles, Bert 57
Coventry blitz 62–3

Currie, Bob 34

Daimler SP250 127
Docker, Sir Bernard 126
Dolomite 44
du Cros, Arthur 15
    Harvey 14
Dunlop, J B 14
Dunlop Tyre Co Ltd 14–15

Eustace, Brian 144

Fearon, Bob 115
FIM 116
Fridlander, A E 14, 15

Gloria Dolomite 40

Halford, Frank 28
Haswell, J R 23
Hathaway, Charles 16, 22
Headlam, Eric 47, 54
Healey, Donald 44
Hele, Doug 132
Hillman, Herbert & Cooper Ltd 13
Holbrook, Claude Vivian 4, 16, 17, 20, 21, 43
Holland, Harry 100, 133

Hopwood, Bert 46, 56, 102, 129, 132
horizontal spring fork 22, 31

Institution of Automobile Engineers Lecture
    (Turner) 91–5
ISDT 104
Isle of Man (dirty work in) 22, 23
'Ixion' 21

Japanese competition 129–31
Jofeh, Lionel 144
John Griffiths Corporation 15
Johnson, Bill Jnr 5, 67
Johnson Motors 133

Leppan, Bob 143
Lord, Leigh 17

Manx GP 102
Masters, Alec 48, 99
Maudes Trophy 36, 50
Mayor of Coventry 14, 16, 18, 19
McCormack, Denis 88
McDonnell, John 57
Mercer, Jack 88
Meriden 65, 75
Miller, Earl 88
Motorcyclist magazine (USA) 77
Much Park Street 14, 59

nacelle   103, 108
North British Rubber Co   22–3
Norton–Villiers–Triumph (NVT)   147

Page, Val   33, 37, 44, 46
Parker, C W F   98
Perry, Harry   44
Plant, Nan   47
post-war development   91–5
Premier Cycle Co Ltd   13
Priory Street Works   35, 40, 55
Production TT   120, 140
profits and losses   145

record breakers   143
Ricardo, Sir Harry   28, 32
Rover Cycle Co Ltd   13

Sangster, J Y   4, 5, 12, 17, 40, 41, 42, 80,
    126, 127, 129, 145
Schulte, Mauritz Johann   4, 13, 15, 16, 21–4
    Muriel   23
Scholefield Goodman & Sons Ltd   76
Scobie, Alex   110
Scottish Six Days Trial   115
Shilton, Neale   156
Simms Bosch Magneto   21
Slippery Sam   142
spring wheel   120
Starley, J K   13
Sturgeon, Harry   132, 136, 144
Sturmey-Archer 3-speed gear   21
SU Carburettor   109
Super Seven car   20

Tait, Percy   110
Thruxton 500   120
'Tin Tabernacle'   63
Triumph Corporation   87
    Engineering Co Ltd   17, 40
Triumph Cycle Co Ltd   14
Triumph models
    Bandit   134, 135
    Bonneville   118–21
    Model CN   36
    Daytona   136–39
    Daytona 750   151, 152
    Daytona 1000   152
    Early models   21, 24–6
    Grand Prix   102
    Junior   31, 34, 110
    Model H   21, 27, 34
    Model LS   31, 32
    Model P   29, 30, 49
    Prototype twin engine   33
    Ricardo   28
    Model SD   28, 34
    Model ST   32, 33
    Speed Twin   49–55, 60, 66, 79, 96, 97,
        103, 118
    Terrier   110, 112, 113, 115
    Thunderbird   105, 108
    Tiger Cub   113–16
    Tiger 70, 80 and 90   48, 58
    Tiger 85   100, 101
    Tiger 100   58, 59, 66, 96, 102, 103
    Tiger 110   110
    Tigress   122, 123
    Tina   123–5
    Model T10   125
    Trident   139–42

Trident 750   152
Trident 900   152
Trophy   104, 107
Trophy 900   152
Trophy 1200   152
Twenty-one   117, 118
Villiers   110
Model X05/1   110
Model X05/5   110
Model 3HW   64, 65
Model 3T de Luxe   96, 99, 103
Model 3TU   95
Model 3TW   61, 62
Model 2/1   39, 48
Model 2/5   37
Model 5/2   38, 39
Model 6/1   36, 39
Triumph name   13
Truslove, Stan   153
Trusty Triumph   21
Tubb, Syd   57
Turner, Edward   4, 5, 33, 42–7, 96, 127,
    133, 135
Turner, Eric   41, 122, 145
TWN (Triumph Werke Nuremberg)   42

Vale, Henry   52

war production   65
Welton, Jack   99
White, Percival   88
White Sewing Machine Co   12, 15
Wickes, Jack   105
world records   116
World War II   60